MILEAGE PRO

BY RANDY PETERSEN & TIM WINSHIP

MILEAGE PRO

The Insider's Guide to
Frequent Flyer
Programs

OAG.

Manufactured in the United States of America.

Limitation of Liability: The authors and the publisher have used their best efforts in collecting and preparing materials for inclusion in *Mileage Pro* but cannot warrant that the information contained in *Mileage Pro* is complete or accurate and do not assume and hereby disclaim liability to any person for any loss or damage caused by errors or omissions in *Mileage Pro* whether such errors or omissions result from negligence, accident or any other cause.

ISBN: 0-9776295-0-3

Cover Design, Layout, Illustrations: Osborn & DeLong, Bloomington, IL

Editor and Associate Publisher: Lisa A. Davis, OAG Worldwide Inc., Downers Grove, IL

Publisher: Kathy Marr, OAG Worldwide Inc., Downers Grove, IL

Inquiries regarding permission for use of material contained in this book, and information on publicity or author interviews should be addressed to:

OAG Worldwide Inc. (Editorial Department)
3025 Highland Parkway
Suite 200
Downers Grove, IL 60515
Tele: 630-515-3206
Fax: 630-515-3251
E-Mail: ladavis@oag.com or MPeditor@oag.com

Mileage Pro is available in bulk for a discounted price.
For more information, go to www.mileageprobook.com or call 1-800-DIALOAG (1-800-342-5624); 1-630-515-5307 (for countries outside the United States and Canada).

Contents

Acknowledgements

In attempting to compile a roster of individuals who played important parts in bringing this book to life it quickly became apparent that even a list that ran tediously long (as ours would) would still be incomplete. Nevertheless, we felt it important to recognize the contribution of others without whose inspiration, knowledge and advice you would not be reading these words.

First, our readers. In our daily interaction with subscribers to our publications we are constantly inspired, challenged and informed. This book is part of that ongoing conversation.

Second, the individuals who design and manage the travel industry's loyalty programs. They are a particularly bright group and the programs themselves are ample evidence of that as is the additional proof of regular contact we have with the program managers and their staff. They keep us on our toes just as we, hopefully, play some small part in keeping them on theirs.

Our thanks as well to the editorial and publishing team at OAG whose dedication to the frequent traveler community and faith in this book was critical in going from book concept to book reality.

And of course, a project like this would be impossible without the love and support of family and friends.

Humble and heartfelt thanks to all.

Randy Petersen
Colorado Springs, Colorado

Tim Winship
Los Angeles, California

Your Welcome Kit

Frequent flyer programs are big, big, BIG.

Big numbers. Big business. Big emotions.

Consider these statistics:

- Worldwide, 163 million travelers are enrolled in more than 130 airline mileage programs. In the United States alone the programs boast 112 million members.

- In 2004, airlines issued 20 million free tickets to U.S. program members in exchange for miles. Even then, almost 10 trillion miles remain in program members' accounts.

- Hotel loyalty programs are almost as popular with some 57 million people belonging to at least one. Hotel programs give away plenty of free room nights. In 2000, there were 3.5 million free hotel room nights. And in 2004, that number grew to more than 5 million. But

A word about terminology. In keeping with the conventions in the frequent traveler community, as well as in the interest of brevity, we often use "miles" to refer to any and all travel loyalty currencies, including airline miles, hotel points and credit card points and miles. Similarly, we use "frequent flyer program" to refer to rewards (also called awards) programs operated by hotels, rental car companies and some credit card issuers, as well as the airline-hosted programs.

there is something more interesting about hotel
programs: About 30 percent of all hotel awards
are converted into airline frequent flyer miles.

All these numbers, and the problems and opportunities they
offer, will increase appreciably in the coming years.

With so many program members invested in so many miles
and points in so many programs, it is no wonder that frequent
flyer programs are a hot topic. They are discussed around the
company water cooler, debated at the dinner table, contested
in divorce proceedings, taxed by the U.S. government, and
obsessed over by millions of people when airlines teeter on the
brink of insolvency.

We could go on, but if you are reading *Mileage Pro* we probably do not need to convince you that travel rewards programs are
a subject worth your attention and energy.

Welcome to our world, the world of miles and points.

Staying on Track

The appeal of rewards programs is obvious: upgrades, flights,
car rentals and hotel stays, all absolutely free. But they are not
without a price. Today, many consumers complain they have to
earn their rewards twice—once by accumulating the necessary
miles or points and again by tracking the various programs'
shifting rules and requirements.

Do more miles, points and memberships guarantee you free
trips? Not always. Many rewards go unredeemed because travelers
either do not have the time to use them or have not learned how
to manage them. Other travelers do not concentrate their loyalty,
finding themselves with miles and points scattered everywhere
except in the program from which they are seeking free travel.

These are just some of the challenges mileage earners face every day. And they are among the reasons you bought this book. If you are struggling with mileage programs, or want to elevate your status as a program participant from intermediate to expert, you have come to the right place. This entire book is devoted to just that.

Expert Help

Welcome to *Mileage Pro*.

For 24 years, members of frequent flyer programs have been trying to make sense of these deceptively simple yet endlessly complicated programs. And, for the most part, they have done it on their own. For the first time, two of the world's most knowledgeable people on the topic of travel rewards programs have combined their extensive advice to produce a "how to" guide for mileage and hotel program participants.

We are Randy Petersen and Tim Winship. And while we spend our days talking miles and points to competing subsets of the frequent flyer universe, we have come together to bring you the most comprehensive and informative book to date on this topic.

Mileage earners come in all shapes and sizes: grizzled road warriors, sun-seeking retirees and budget-conscious young adults. To an extent never envisioned in their early days, today's frequent flyer programs offer real value for consumers in almost every segment of the demographic spectrum.

For those who travel less than they would like, airline programs can be a rich source of free tickets. While travel remains among the best ways to earn miles, it is no longer a necessary part of the equation. Free flights can be had without earning a single mile through paid flights or hotel stays. As discussed in some detail in this book, frequent flyer programs have truly evolved into frequent buyer programs through credit card purchases and such.

If you already spend more time traveling than you do staying at home, frequent flyer programs can be the principal means— in many cases the only means—of obtaining upgrades and other perks designed specifically to moderate the stress and discomfort associated with life on the road.

We Dedicate This Book to ...

We have aimed this book squarely at the middle level of the mileage earning community because there are more of you and because there is more to be gained from educating the mainstream. But mileage novices and veterans alike will discover new advice and tips as well.

Beginners should read this book as a primer; a survey of the basic concepts and terminology associated with frequent flyer programs plus an introduction to strategies and tactics for intelligently using the programs. In addition to the "how to" aspects, the programs' historical and business contexts are also discussed.

For those at the very top of the knowledge and experience pyramid, much of our advice will be more of a reminder than a revelation. (If it is not, it should be.) So, consider *Mileage Pro* a refresher; a veritable reality check against your current assumptions and practices. For more specific information and advice— much of which is time sensitive and therefore not well suited to a book's static format—we have included a resources section on page 183 with Web site addresses and other publications.

Straight Talk

As much as any of our fellow travelers have groaned at some of the changes that have been imposed on frequent flyer programs in years past, so have we. We each have been known to offer a stern comment or two in response to changes that have negatively affected the value of "loyalty." As well, we have both cheered for developments that have made these programs richly rewarding—at least to those well-informed members who abide by a few basic principles. These programs continue to confound cynics who declared them not worthy of your membership, too expensive for airlines and hotels to operate, and likely victims of the days that followed 9/11.

We wrote this book in response to what we see as a lack of reliable, no-nonsense information for travelers interested in leveraging their frequent flyer program memberships to squeeze every ounce of value from their trips and purchases. We wrote it to clear up misconceptions, to help you understand the inner workings of the programs and to steer you clear of the mistakes that can easily be made when choosing the wrong program or misusing the right program. And we wrote it because, frankly, we could not imagine not writing it.

Joint Venture

In the very small world of publishing news and advice for frequent flyer program aficionados, Randy and Tim are competitors. So, the initial response from those who first learned Randy and Tim were collaborating on this book was, "What, sleeping with the enemy?" One wag likened the partnership to American and United putting aside their long-running war to...

well, he could not imagine those two airlines cooperating on much of anything.

That competition may be a fact of life in the airline industry but in a publishing venture with a consumer advocacy focus, we felt that two heads truly would be better than one.

While either Randy or Tim could have written a good book on the subject of frequent flyer programs, it would not be this book. More importantly, it would not be as good as this book; it would not be as comprehensive, as insightful and as helpful. And that was the point of joining forces: to produce a book that respects our readers by doing justice to the subject of frequent flyer programs.

We are confident that a deeper understanding of these ingenious programs will make participating in them not only more rewarding but also more entertaining.

MEMORABLE MOMENTS OF MILES & POINTS

JANUARY 2005

As the year began, **the world's frequent flyer programs** boasted more than 163 million members, 112 million of whom were U.S. residents. In the accounts of those members: an astounding 10 trillion outstanding miles.

We get up every morning looking forward to a new day of developments in the world of miles and points. We are rarely disappointed. If, after reading *Mileage Pro,* you understand our enthusiasm, this book will have succeeded. If you share our enthusiasm, it will have succeeded beyond our expectations.

Chapter 1

The Birth of Frequent Flyer Programs

SURPRISINGLY, THE PRECURSOR TO VALUING miles was valuing stamps.

Remember those books bulging with S&H Green Stamps squirreled away in kitchen drawers and in your mom's purse? Recall the Green Stamps award catalog displayed on the living room table alongside the latest issues of *Life* and *Look?*

This legendary Green Stamps scheme was based on a now-familiar proposition: Confine your purchases to a select group of retailers such as grocery stores, department stores and gas stations, and, in return for your loyalty, receive a reward.

Some consumers thought of the rewards—principally hard goods such as radios, bicycles and kitchenware—as gifts. Others factored them into their shopping calculations as rebates. Either way, the stamps proved to be a powerful currency, and ultimately were redeemed for more than $10 billion in merchandise.

How big a deal were Green Stamps? According to S&H (which today operates an electronic version of the program called Greenpoints), in the heyday of Green Stamps, S&H was printing three times as many stamps as that of the United States Post Office. And the S&H rewards catalog was the country's largest publication.

To an unprecedented extent, Green Stamps trained shoppers to expect their loyalty to be systematically rewarded.

Mileage Programs Take Off

It was not until May 1981 that American Airlines attempted to capitalize on that expectation with the launch of the first mileage-based airline loyalty program, AAdvantage.

[Sidenote: While American was the first airline to reward customers with miles, it was not the first to launch a customer rewards program. In 1979, Western Airlines started a simple rewards program, Travel Pass, which has a legitimate claim as one of the direct ancestors of today's loyalty programs. Designed with business travelers in mind, Travel Pass rewarded customers with a $50 travel certificate after they completed five Western flights. Other pre-AAdvantage programs included the Executive Air Travel program from United Airlines, the Flying Colonel program from Delta Air Lines and the Alaska Aeronaut program from Alaska Airlines. Recognition was often in the form of a personalized plaque engraved with the member's name. Members were able to add to their plaques receiving metal markers listing the names of the cities to which they flew most often. With no fancy Platinum cards or upgrades, members proudly displayed these mementos in their offices while many also formed personal relationships with their preferred airline's local city managers.]

American, under the leadership of Robert Crandall, had already established itself as an industry leader in both technology and marketing. And AAdvantage leveraged both those competencies.

According to Crandall, "We did a lot of careful research, which established that travel was on every consumer's priority list of wants. Thus, we thought that a travel-based reward program would be very attractive to our customers and would eventually be a good distribution channel. Both turned out to be correct."

Once AAdvantage's design was in place, American drew from its Admirals Clubs and American Traveler membership lists, pre-enrolling just under 200,000 charter members.

According to American insiders, Crandall himself was only peripherally involved with the development of AAdvantage. Most of the credit goes to a handful of Crandall's lieutenants, including Tom Plaskett, senior vice president of sales and marketing, Nick Babounakis, director of marketing plans, Rolfe Shellenberger, manager of marketing plans, and consultant Hal Brierley.

American quickly realized its mileage program was more efficient than mass-market advertising and was more cost effective. In the early days of AAdvantage, American boasted that their new rewards program saved the airline millions of dollars in advertising costs.

Meanwhile, in Chicago

While American was a step ahead of other airlines, United had its own program up and running within six days of American's.

Hardly an after-the-fact counter punch, United had already developed its own loyalty program, Mileage Plus, but was dealing with the fallout from a recent union strike and decided to delay deployment.

According to Don Moonjian, United's vice president of market management: "We had gone out some time before that and developed a whole bunch of [loyalty] programs that we basically felt we could use to come back from the strike. At that time, we elected to go with the half-fare coupon because we were looking for something with an immediate response. As [Mileage Plus] was something that would build over time, we said, 'OK, we are going to go with the half-fare coupon and let's put this frequent flyer thing on the side in case we need something else further down the line.' Then lo and behold, not long after that American came out with AAdvantage and we basically pulled that thing off the shelf, dusted it off, called it Mileage Plus, and put it to work."

The "Plus" in Mileage Plus referred to United's principal strategy for offsetting American's first-mover advantage: a 5,000-mile enrollment bonus for new members.

Proliferation of Partnerships

American understood from the beginning that flights were just one component of the total travel package. So, in the first year they expanded AAdvantage to allow members to earn and redeem miles for car rentals from Hertz and from hotel stays at Hyatt.

Through the years, American continually expanded their partner roster, initially to include more travel suppliers and later to include non-travel categories. Today, AAdvantage boasts more than 1,200 partner companies affording AAdvantage members opportunities to earn miles for everything from buying groceries to financing a home to accruing a retirement fund.

Partnerships are not only an important part of a loyalty program's success as a marketing scheme, they are also key to a program's evolution into a large and very profitable business.

Hotels Launch Programs

Most hotels were first exposed to loyalty programs through their participation as partners in one or more of the airline programs. That experience was more than enough to convince them of the power of "loyalty" and to suggest the possibility of launching programs of their own.

In January 1983, Holiday Inn was the first to deploy its own frequent stay program, Priority Club.

As often happens to trailblazers, Holiday Inn's first attempt included missteps. In particular, the award side of the program was insupportably generous rewarding members with two free airline tickets to Europe, one week's hotel stay in Paris, and a week's free car rental after just 75 stays. Not surprisingly, in 1986, Priority Club shut down under cost pressure. The ratio of revenue to benefits was recalibrated and a new program was launched several months later.

Marriott introduced its program, Honored Guest Awards (now Marriott Rewards), in November 1983, but it was not until June 1986 when the third hotel program was unveiled, Sheraton's Club International. Two major programs debuted in 1987: Westin Premier in January and Hilton HHonors in May.

Today, all larger hotel chains (such as InterContinental Hotels Group, which includes InterContinental, Staybridge Suites, Holiday Inn and Crowne Plaza) have their own frequent stay programs. (The program's size is deemed a competitive advantage insofar as larger numbers of participating hotels make it that much easier for travelers to concentrate their stays within a chain's network.)

Through their respective families of brands, Priority Club Rewards (InterContinental Hotels Group) has a network of 3,400

INTERESTING FACT: Hilton's HHonors program—which went on to break new ground with such innovations as Double Dipping (awarding both hotel points and airline miles for the same stay) and Rewards Exchange (allowing both points-to-miles and miles-to-points conversions)—began life as both a frequent stay program and a fundraiser for the 1988 U.S. Olympic team. Each time a HHonors member checked into a Hilton, the company made a donation to support Olympic athletes. The initiative netted more than one million dollars in contributions and the Olympics Association gave rise to the now standard naming convention for loyalty program elite tiers: Bronze, Silver and Gold.

participating hotels; Hilton HHonors has 2,700; Marriott Rewards has 2,500; and Starwood Preferred Guest (St. Regis, The Luxury Collection, Sheraton, W, Westin and Four Points) has 725.

Driving Deals

While airline and hotel loyalty programs have grown steadily, rental car companies' enthusiasm for rewards programs has been a decidedly up and down affair.

Since 1987 when National Car Rental introduced the first frequent renter program called Emerald Club, rental car companies have tested a host of program approaches. They have experimented with airline miles, proprietary points, membership fees and value-added services, among others.

Almost as variable has been the rental companies' attitude toward participating in the airlines' programs. The source of their ambivalence is nothing less than the answer to a fundamental marketing question: If all companies in the rental car industry offer miles in virtually all major airline programs, is it worth the extra costs to offer an incentive that no longer provides a competitive advantage?

In the absence of a clear answer—positive or negative—the car companies often seem to feel they are being held hostage by the airlines, grudgingly paying extra for miles just to maintain a level playing field. Because the airlines believe car rental companies get extra business from the airlines' mileage incentive programs, the airlines charge the car rental companies for the miles.

In 1997, in response to the newly announced 7.5 percent Federal Excise Tax imposed on partners purchasing miles from airlines, Frank Olson, Hertz's former CEO, complained very publicly that the costs to award miles had become insupportable. His remarks were widely interpreted as a signal to competitors that Hertz was ready to withdraw from its airline tie-ups if other rental car companies would do the same. There was no mass exodus and Hertz now assesses customers a surcharge on rentals that earn miles to partially offset the federal tax.

Going Global

The success of U.S. airlines' loyalty programs soon caught the attention of foreign carriers. This often began with complaints from sales reps and reservations agents that they were losing prospective customers to American carriers on the strength of the carriers' mileage incentives.

Asian and European airlines had not shown great enthusiasm for the new U.S. marketing programs viewing them as crass rebate schemes or low class tactics fundamentally incompatible with their high class products.

They preferred to compete on service, selling their wares with soft-focused magazine ads depicting fetching flight attendants serving three-star meals to passengers stretched out in kingly splendor.

Due to the significance of transatlantic traffic to its overall revenue, and perhaps to cultural affinities as well, British Airways was the first non-U.S. airline to partner with a U.S. mileage program, affiliating itself with American's AAdvantage program in 1982.

Today, almost all of the world's airlines operate their own programs, or participate in the programs of other carriers, either bilaterally or multilaterally via comprehensive global alliances.

Plastic Plans

The miles-for-charges phenomenon began in October 1985 with Diners Club's launch of Club Rewards. Members were awarded Club Rewards points for purchases made with the Diners Club card; the points could then be redeemed for miles and points in the programs of participating airlines and hotels. (Because Club Rewards points—and later, points in the American Express Membership Rewards program—could be exchanged for miles and points in multiple loyalty programs, they became known as convertible currencies.)

The world had to wait another year for what would be the first of many credit cards to be uniquely associated with a specific airline program, including the Continental TravelBank Gold MasterCard, which was first issued in November 1986. Holiday Inn Priority Club launched the first hotel affinity card in April 1987. And in June of the same year, American rolled out co-branded AAdvantage MasterCard and Visa cards issued by Citibank. The current AAdvantage MasterCard is the world's most popular affinity card.

Today, almost every significant airline and hotel program has its own co-branded credit card. Credit cards are by far the largest contributor to travelers' mileage accounts after miles for flying.

From Flyers to Buyers

The evolution of frequent flyer programs into frequent buyer programs began early in the history of mileage programs with the introduction of mileage earning credit cards.

In fact, it was the early days of Internet retailing that jump-started shopping miles. Online merchants such as Barnes and Noble and The Gap, seeking ways to differentiate themselves from competitors with comparable products and prices, offered customers airline miles as well as points from such Web-based loyalty programs as ClickRewards, MyPoints and Green Points.

It is estimated that as a group, U.S. airlines sell more than four billion dollars per year in frequent flyer miles.

Online commerce lends itself particularly well to loyalty programs because the transactions are computer based, making the transfer of tracking information from the retailer to the mileage program's database a relatively straightforward proposition.

In 2000, when the Internet bubble burst, many Web-based loyalty program issuers were wiped out, joining Pets.com and Webvan in the ditch alongside the electronic highway. Consumer interest (and faith) in those that survived dropped off dramatically. The loyalty currency that survived the shakeout was the old standby: airline miles.

Money Talks

With their long lists of partners, each of which purchases miles from the airlines at one to two cents per mile, frequent flyer programs have become big businesses unto themselves—and very profitable ones at that.

American Airlines alone generates annual revenues of one billion dollars from the sale of frequent flyer miles to AAdvantage program partners, including Citibank (which issues the AAdvantage MasterCard), all major hotel and rental car chains, more than 30 other airlines and 1,200 additional companies such as Flowers.com that use AAdvantage miles to spur additional sales of their products and services.

Contrary to popular belief, the costs of operating the programs are relatively modest. In particular, the expenses associated with a free award ticket are far less than the perceived value of the

MEMORABLE MOMENTS
OF MILES & POINTS

MAY 1981

American Airlines introduces AAdvantage, the first mileage-based frequent flyer program. Within a matter of days, United launches its own program, Mileage Plus.

ticket. Because an airline's sophisticated yield management software so precisely limits seats for award use that would have gone unsold anyway, the only expense to the airline in fulfilling an award request are the direct costs of flying one additional passenger, including extra jet fuel, insurance and meal service. According to the carriers' 10-K reports, those costs are a paltry $10 to $50 per award ticket.

Consumers do not much care about the economics underlying mileage programs nor should they. But recognizing the programs' power to generate profits gives the lie to one of the recurring rumors among travelers: That the airlines rue the day they launched the programs and that they will terminate them as soon as the competitive situation allows.

Kill the goose that lays the golden egg? Not likely.

In fact, the joke among travel industry insiders is that loyalty programs have become the airlines' primary business, relegating air transportation to a subsidiary role. While that characterization somewhat overstates the case, it does point out the fundamental irony of the situation.

Mileage programs will remain a fixture in the industry for the foreseeable future. As far as earning and burning miles goes, consumers can strap themselves in for a long—albeit occasionally bumpy—ride.

⊕ REMEMBER THIS:

- American Airlines launched AAdvantage, the first modern frequent flyer program, in 1981. Today, 163 million travelers are enrolled in more than 130 airline mileage programs worldwide.

- Originally targeted to frequent flyers, the programs now cater to frequent buyers as well.

- Loyalty programs generate significant revenues for the airlines that host them. So, contrary to popular opinion, the airlines have no reason to terminate the programs. Rest assured: Mileage programs will be with us for years to come.

Chapter 2

Frequent Flyer 101

AS ANY TRAVEL MARKETER WILL tell you, airline frequent flyer programs are designed to gain and retain the business of travelers by rewarding them for their loyalty.

Very much like how a neighborhood coffee house rewards patrons with a free cup of Joe after they purchase 12, frequent flyer programs attempt to keep customers coming back for more by promising them free trips and other perks after they meet certain conditions.

The airlines have taken the concept of loyalty programs (also called frequency programs, rewards programs, mileage programs and customer relationship management programs) to levels of size, sophistication and value unmatched outside the travel sector.

Actually, there is more to travel loyalty programs than the airlines' schemes. While first offered by airlines, these programs are now equally endorsed and popular among hotel chains and credit card companies, and to a lesser extent by rental car companies. Because of the popularity of these programs, and because these programs use both miles and points, the term "frequent flyer" when used throughout this book refers to travel loyalty programs in general.

There are essentially two types of members who commit to frequent flyer programs: The frequent business traveler for whom these programs were first introduced (and who still represent the greatest share of revenue for the airlines) and the mileage consumer who might best be described as an "infrequent" flyer who enjoys accumulating miles by patronizing the airlines' various partners. The frequent business traveler is rewarded with a wealth of benefits including free upgrades and earning elite status, which is most often offered in tiers: Usually gold and platinum, though almost any precious metal or mineral (think diamonds, rubies and sapphires) might apply.

Much like dollars in a bank, your frequent flyer miles reside in your account. Miles accumulate as you travel, but unfortunately they do not earn interest. At present, most of the larger domestic airlines use a fairly uniform policy: Your earned miles will not expire if you have activity in your account once every three years. The type of activity varies between programs, but generally any activity—including redeeming an award or using a partner—will suffice in making your miles active. When the mileage total reaches a certain amount, you can "redeem" it for an award, usually free travel.

Airline Programs

The common currency among airline programs is miles. However, some programs still award points or credits instead of miles. Most airline programs award miles based on the actual miles flown. For example, the flight distance between Los Angeles and Dallas is 1,235 miles; therefore, a traveler flying roundtrip between Los Angeles and Dallas will earn 2,470 miles toward an award.

Once enough miles are earned (20,000 to 30,000 in most programs) the miles may be exchanged for a free ticket. An upgrade to business or first class usually starts at 10,000 miles.

Members of frequent flyer programs should also be aware of minimum miles, class-of-service bonuses and partner miles.

Minimum miles: Some programs award minimum mileage regardless of the actual miles flown. For example, on flights that are 500 miles or less, some airlines award 500 miles.

Class-of-service bonuses: With some airline programs, when a first class ticket is purchased, the traveler will receive a bonus equal to 50 percent of the actual miles flown. Class-of-service bonuses may also be awarded for business class travel.

Partner miles: Airlines also award miles for hotel stays, car rentals, credit card purchases, long distance telephone calls and flower purchases. Businesses that award airline miles are referred to as "partners."

Hotel Programs

Hotel frequent guest programs vary greatly in the manner in which points are earned and in the types of awards that are available.

The common currency among hotel programs is points. Generally, hotels award points based on the dollar amount of room charges per stay. For example, guests will earn 10 points per one dollar charged to the room. Eligible charges may include room rate, food and beverage (including room service), telephone and laundry. Or, guests may earn points based on the stay only. For example, the hotel may award 500 points per stay (regardless of whether the stay is for one night or five nights).

Many hotel programs give guests the option of earning points valid for redemption in the hotel's program OR miles valid for redemption in an airline program. A few hotel programs (such as Hilton HHonors) award both hotel points and miles (this is called double dipping). So, for example, a HHonors member can elect to receive both HHonors points and miles in one of 55 participating airline programs.

Note: A flight in conjunction with a hotel stay may be required by the airline or hotel in order for the hotel stay to be eligible to earn miles.

MEMORABLE MOMENTS
OF MILES & POINTS

NOVEMBER 1981
American launched the first frequent flyer program promotion, the "AA Holiday Special," for travel between November 15, 1981 and January 31, 1982. The offer: Fly 7,000 miles with a minimum of five flight segments to earn a free first class ticket to any American Airlines destination. In those days, the airline did not fly globally like it does today, and the free award certificates were redeemable at travel agencies.

Hotel program points can also be earned for partner car rentals and partner credit card purchases.

Car Rental Programs

For frequent travelers, car rentals are known primarily as a source of airline miles or hotel points. For example, members of frequent car programs may earn 50 miles per rental. A flight or stay in conjunction with the car rental may be required by the airline or hotel in order for the rental to be eligible to earn miles or points. A few car rental agencies do offer frequent renter programs of their own. Generally, the programs are quite simple. For example, Hertz awards travelers a free rental day after 12 rentals.

Credit Card Programs

Credit card programs award miles or points based on purchases. There are two types of credit card programs: 1) Affinity credit cards such as the Continental Airlines World MasterCard and the Marriot Rewards Visa, both issued by Chase. These sorts of cards are directly connected to an airline or hotel program (thus "affinity"). Miles or points are awarded per dollar spent and then deposited monthly into the member's loyalty program account. 2) Credit cards operate programs of their own and points are awarded per dollar spent. Points can be redeemed for miles or points in an airline or hotel program, or they can be redeemed for awards offered by the credit card program itself. See chapter 5 (Plastic Magic: Credit Card Miles and Points) on page 43 for more information on credit card award options.

Many credit cards impose caps on the number of miles annually earned. For example, the popular American AAdvantage MasterCard issued by Citibank has annual maximums (waived for elite members) of 60,000 for Gold and 100,000 for Platinum cards respectively.

Partners

Airline and hotel programs have established a network of partners that award miles or points. Some programs even award miles for flower purchases, moving services and investments in mutual funds.

Partnerships are an excellent way for someone who flies only occasionally to supplement his or her loyalty program account. In theory, a free flight can be earned solely through the use of program partners. For example, if you charge all of your purchases to an airline affinity credit card and sign up with a partner long distance carrier, depending upon your level of activity, you could earn an airline award in 12 months. The proliferation of partnerships has made it much easier to earn free travel awards, particularly with programs that enforce the expiration of miles and points since partner activity is considered enough activity to keep an account active.

Planning

One of the most important aspects of loyalty membership is careful planning to ensure you accumulate the most miles and points. Read through the information in your loyalty program's newsletter to ensure you are earning the most miles and points possible. For example, if you are traveling to Chicago and one of your hotel programs is offering a limited-time 100 percent bonus, all other things being equal, it is in your best interest to stay at the hotel that will give you the most points.

Consider this scenario: You are taking a three-day trip from Chicago to Los Angeles (Sunday through Tuesday). You fly United (earning 3,490 miles), stay at the J.W. Marriott (earning 500 miles), and rent from Hertz (50 more miles). Your total for the trip is 4,040 miles. With better planning, you might have chosen Delta instead of United. Delta was offering a 1,000-mile connection bonus through Denver and another bonus of 2,000 miles for flights Sunday through Friday, thus you would have earned 7,500 total miles for the flight. You could have earned even more miles using some of Delta's hotel and car rental partners. For instance, you could have stayed at the Los Angeles Airport Marriott on Sunday night for 1,000 bonus miles and then switched to the J.W. Marriott on Monday night for an additional 1,000 bonus miles. At the airport, you would have rented from Avis on Sunday and earned 100 bonus miles, then turned the car in on Monday morning and switched to Hertz for another 100 miles. Ultimately, choosing Delta and its partners would have been worth 11,500 miles (156 percent more than the original trip). (In this case Delta was preferable to United; under different circumstances, of course, the choice might be the opposite.) By using an airline affinity credit card to purchase the tickets and pay for the hotels, car rentals and dinners, you could have added another 2,000 miles. You could have added even more miles by using a long distance telephone service (program partner) for your calls back to the office.

Recordkeeping

An estimated 7 to 8 percent of all travel is improperly recorded. Do not expect the airlines, hotels and car rental companies to be sympathetic. As in real life, a thousand things can go wrong, and often do. We suggest you pay attention to the following:

Retain Records and Receipts
Keep track of mileage earned and check it against the statement your program provides. Keep boarding passes and passenger coupon portions of tickets. Keep an accounting log for withdrawals and deposits much like you do with your check registry. If you have to submit expense reports for travel, always make copies of receipts before submitting the necessary paperwork to

your company. Keep track of special promotions in which you are participating as not all programs will account for double miles and points when replacing missing credit.

Policies and Procedures

Check your airline's policies concerning inter-line reciprocity, changing tickets and re-crediting mileage for unused tickets. If you were bumped from a canceled flight onto another airline, you will want to know your airline's policy for awarding credit for that flight. Make sure your travel agent has on file your frequent traveler membership numbers. Make a list of the retroactive dates for each of your programs. Some will not let you file for missing credit more than three to six months after the date of travel. Others, such as American AAdvantage, will let you file for missing credit up to 12 months later as long as you were a member of the program when the credit was not posted.

Elite Status

If we could give one piece of advice to every frequent traveler it is this: Accumulate as many miles and achieve as high a status as possible with various frequent flyer programs. Often called elite-level programs, we are referring to the level of membership at which you can earn the most miles, points and privileges. Although some programs still have not introduced higher levels of membership, elite status is indeed a standard in the industry.

Some people might wonder why we suggest going out of your way to pay for and travel on another trip just to qualify for elite level membership. Review the various elite level programs offered by your airline or hotel and you will see why this is an important decision. Most provide special upgrades at no cost as well as tier bonuses that can increase your mileage and point totals automatically by 25 to 125 percent each time you travel. For most members, that means a 25,000-mile free award can be earned with only 12,500 actual flight miles, even with no partner bonuses.

Each December, you should make a point of reviewing your mileage totals with your major programs and decide which benefits you want to have for the next year. Trust us, as a Gold, Premier, Platinum or other elite level member, you will be treated differently.

The Bottom Line

Loyalty programs work whether you travel regularly or just occasionally, and even if you do not have elite status. A little more graciousness and cooperation seem to be extended to members of loyalty programs by the personnel at airline ticket counters, hotel registration desks and car rental counters. Members of Northwest WorldPerks program often receive special airfare offers not available to the general public, and most hotel guest programs allow members, even basic members, such privileges as free gym use and daily newspapers.

⊕ REMEMBER THIS:

◈ There are essentially two types of members to frequent flyer programs: the frequent business traveler and the "mileage consumer." The frequent business traveler flies to earn most of his or her miles, whereas the mileage consumer is the more infrequent flyer earning most of his or her miles from the airline's partners, such as grocery stores and restaurants.

◈ Did you know that an estimated 7 to 8 percent of all travel is improperly recorded? Recordkeeping is a must for those who do more than just fly when earning their miles.

◈ Tier bonuses are one of the most important benefits of earning elite-level status. Mid-tier members often earn a 100 percent bonus from their flights, meaning they only need to fly 12,500 miles to earn a 25,000-mile award.

Chapter 3

Choosing a Program Made Simple

FOR THE MAJORITY OF TRAVELERS—those who fly either occasionally or moderately—often the goal of earning miles is a free trip. For true frequent flyers—the programs' top 10 percent, typically business travelers—the lure of a free trip takes a back seat to the benefits of earning elite status, including upgrades, priority boarding and other perks designed to soften the hard edges of life on the road.

Whether it is an award ticket or elite status, frequent flyer miles only have value when a program participant has accumulated enough miles to reach an award threshold. In most programs, domestic coach awards require 25,000 miles and entry-level elite status is earned for flying 25,000 elite qualifying miles during a calendar year.

Since combining miles in most programs is not allowed, 25,000 miles spread among multiple programs prove to be effectively worthless. On the other hand, if all 25,000 miles had been earned in a single program, the member could cash in for a free ticket and possibly reach elite status. As noted, elite status is granted if the miles were earned within a calendar year, including miles earned on elite qualifying partner carriers.

Comparing the value of miles divided among numerous programs to the value of miles consolidated in just one program highlights the importance of earning your miles in a single program.

Here is an example. Let's say you have 4,300 miles in Continental's OnePass program, 8,700 miles in a US Airways Dividend Miles account, and 2,100 miles in a United Mileage Plus account. Individually, you have nothing of value to use toward a free trip. However, had you diligently earned these same miles (a total of 15,100) with a single airline, you would probably be eligible for a free airline ticket. (Say you had chosen United as your preferred airline, you could have taken advantage of their current ticket award offer of 15,000 miles.)

Choose 'Em and Use 'Em

Since there is no cost to join a loyalty program, the natural tendency is to sign up for each and every program of each and every airline, hotel and rental car company you patronize. But that leads to award dilution—many miles but few actual awards. And monitoring and managing participation in a multitude of programs can be a real time killer as well.

The key to maximizing awards is picking one program and, as much as possible, confining your mileage earning within that program's network of partners. Which program to choose? It is not a matter of comparing airline programs and ranking them according to the most robust lineup of partners, or the best record of accommodating award requests. The best program is the one that best fits your existing travel and shopping patterns. It is the one that awards you the most miles for the most transactions at the least cost and with the least inconvenience.

As for those program members who earn the majority of their miles from flying, the best program is the one whose airline partners offer the most flights and the best schedules on the routes most often flown.

If the choice of programs boils down to the choice of airline, the choice of airline is driven by two related considerations: The traveler's hometown airport, which defines the universe of available airlines, and the traveler's habitual flight destinations, which narrows the list further to those airlines serving the desired city pairs.

> The best program is the one that best fits your existing travel and shopping patterns. It is the one that awards you the most miles for the most transactions at the least cost and with the least inconvenience.

The best approach is to join the program hosted by the airline you will be flying most often. Then, concentrate your travel and non-travel purchases with that airline and the airline's partners. The miles and awards will follow.

Tiebreakers

Generally, the combination of a traveler's local airport and customary travel patterns is enough to establish one airline as the best fit for both flying and mileage accumulation. If not, the following information may help narrow the field.

+ *Route coverage* — It used to be the airline program
  with the larger route network trumped the program
  of the carrier with the smaller network simply
  because it is easier to earn miles within a larger
  network than within a smaller one. That remains true
  today, but rather than consider just the program's
  route network, you also want to factor in the extended
  route network created by the airline's participation
  in one of the three global airline alliances: oneworld,
  SkyTeam and Star Alliance. For purposes of earning
  and redeeming miles, and for earning elite status,
  an airline's participation in an alliance can be very
  helpful. Travelers can earn and redeem miles with
  their airline's alliance partners, and they can earn
  additional elite status in the alliance. Another benefit
  when traveling internationally is being able to use
  the alliance partners' airport lounges—as long as the
  traveler has elite status with his or her primary airline
  or has earned elite status with the alliance. (See the
  Using Airline Alliances chapter on page 119 for more
  information on alliances and their relationship to
  mileage programs.)

The ideal airline will cover at least 60 percent of the
cities to which you fly, and its partners in one of the
global alliances will be in line with your other travel
needs. If you travel to Europe once or twice a year, make
sure your airline, or one of your airline's international
partners, covers that distance. You will miss too many
miles if you do not choose wisely in the beginning.

- *Program partnerships* — Just as a program's network of airline partners translates into opportunities to earn more miles and take award trips almost anywhere in the world, the program's non-airline partners also enlarge the universe of opportunities to earn miles for, well, just about any transaction that involves an exchange of money for goods or services.

    For example, on a flight from Chicago to Denver, you will earn between 1,500 and 2,000 miles (roundtrip) depending on your airline's program. An affiliated hotel partner can add 500 to 1,000 bonus miles to that total, and a partner car rental can add another 50 to 500 bonus miles.

- *Award availability* — Not all programs are equally generous when it comes to making seats available for award travel or upgrades. Unfortunately, there are no definitive data available on redemption success rates. But it is worth checking with other frequent travelers to see whether competing programs are doing a better or a worse job of meeting member expectations.

- *Mileage expiration* — Loyalty programs of JetBlue and other discount airlines have mileage expiration policies that make their loyalty programs inferior to those of major airlines. In some cases, miles expire after just one or two years, regardless of your activity. For slow but steady earners, programs with these types of expiration policies will only be an exercise in frustration and disappointment.

♦ *Mileage earning rate* — Among airlines, a mile is
a mile. But some airlines offer double and triple
mileage promotions more often than others. During
the past two years, British Airways has offered its
members a chance to earn as much as 50,000 bonus
miles when flying transatlantic during the slower
winter months. Also, when airlines introduce new
route service to an area, they often offer double
miles or triple miles as an incentive. When Alaska
Airlines offered new twice-daily service to Dallas
in September 2005, they offered all their members
double miles for a period of two months.

Hotel programs' earning rates are more difficult to
compare. Some offer ten points per dollar spent,
others five, four or even one. To calculate which
program will allow you to accumulate the most
value for each dollar spent, take the folio amounts
for your last five hotel stays and multiply them by
the spending ratios of each of your top three hotel

Program Accumulation		
Folio amounts of last 5 hotel stays	X Spending ratios of top 3 hotel choices =	Credits earned for each program

choices (within your travel budget), then compare
that amount with the award chart from each hotel's
program. That will give you the rate at which credits
are earned for each program. We suggest leaving
out partner bonuses and relying on the base rate
of earning. Keep in mind that some hotel programs
allow double dipping, earning both hotel points and

airline miles for the same stay. That puts a kink in our equation, but you can at least get an idea of what you are earning.

- *Minimum miles per flight* — If you live in Phoenix and fly regularly to New York for business then skip this advice. But if your travel calendar is typically filled with short hops, minimum mileage is important. For instance, for someone traveling regularly between Chicago and Detroit, a program offering a 750-mile minimum will be 50 percent better than one offering a 500-mile minimum. Do not underestimate the importance of minimum miles.

- *Flight conjunction requirements* — Some hotels and car rental companies require that flights be in conjunction with hotel stays or car rentals in order for members to earn miles.

- *Award transferability* — If you are not married, this might be an important factor. Find out whether you can give awards to anyone you choose, especially a business partner or a friend. There is nothing more frustrating than being the only person eligible to use an award when you have more mileage in your account than you can use.

- *Companion tickets* — Which program has companion tickets at lower mileage requirements that will allow you to take your spouse or children along on a paid business trip?

- *Which upgrades are "fare" to use* — If flying in first class is your favorite benefit, make sure your airline program has a reasonable mileage redemption policy for upgrades and has eligible first class fares that you are willing to pay. If you are flying on discounted coach fares, as most people do, consider only airlines programs that allow you to upgrade from any published fare as opposed to full fares only.

- *Airline stability* — Due to the unstable nature of the airline industry, make sure the airline with which you plan to earn miles is relatively healthy and not on the brink of bankruptcy. When Midway and Braniff airlines went out of business, thousands of frequent travelers lost hundreds of thousands of frequent flyer miles. Given the choice, select an airline that is likely to still be in business when you are ready to use your hard-earned miles.

- *Affinity Credit Cards* — It is almost impossible to travel these days without some kind of credit card. Smart frequent flyers are those who have traded their existing Visa and MasterCard credit cards for cards affiliated with the airline or hotel programs to which they belong. This is not an additional credit card; it simply replaces the one you have. Affinity credit cards offer the same credit privileges as your other credit cards, but in addition to enhanced travel benefits, such as bonus miles and points just for signing up and additional insurance and collision damage waivers for car rentals, they offer the ability to earn one bonus mile or point for every dollar charged to the card.

Make Room for Hotel Programs

Frequent travelers traditionally have supplemented their airline program earnings with points accrued in the frequent guest programs of one or more major hotel chains.

While hotel programs are rarely treated as primary programs, it is handy (and financially prudent) to have enough points in a frequent hotel program to redeem free hotel nights or to combine free stays with free air tickets when constructing a complete travel package.

In fact, as airfares have declined over the past few years hotel rates have risen, thus the hotel portion of a trip's cost has increased. So, there is more reason than ever to make free nights a priority.

As with airline programs, the most effective approach is to choose a hotel program that best fits your travel patterns, such as a program hosted by a hotel chain that has hotel properties at the right price points and in the right locations.

For a time, airline programs offered hotel stays as awards. That practice was discontinued, but seems to be making a cautious comeback with American and United recently restoring hotel nights to their award charts. American charges a fee to redeem miles for hotel awards and United limits them to elite members.

A Place for Charge Cards

Some knowledgeable mileage earners participate in one of the two multi-currency charge card programs, American Express Membership Rewards and Diners Club Rewards. As discussed in greater detail in the credit card chapter on page 43, points earned in the Membership Rewards and Club Rewards programs can be exchanged for miles and points in participating airline and hotel programs.

The strategy is to maintain a cache of these convertible points as a reserve account, to be tapped into when other airline or hotel accounts need topping off to reach an award threshold.

Buyer or Flyer?

Frequent flyer programs have evolved to accommodate a wide spectrum of consumer behavior, from those whose earnings derive exclusively from travel, to those who earn awards solely from shopping.

Along the way, we have seen two notable outbreaks of competing programs, expressly designed to wean the frequent buyer group away from their allegiance to airline programs: Online shopping rewards programs and credit card travel rewards

---

What about frequent buyers who earn the bulk of their miles from shopping? We will look closely at the pros and cons of credit card miles for frequent shoppers in chapter 5. But for now, suffice to say that airline programs trump credit card programs in the most significant respects, most importantly mileage earning power.

programs. Both types of programs are modeled after airline programs, oftentimes awarding miles for transactions (even though there is no travel involved) and featuring airline tickets as awards.

The online shopping rewards programs were early attempts at Internet marketing, with names such as AllAdvantage, Beenz, ClickRewards, CyberGold, DeltaClick, Freeairmiles.com, FreeRide, GiantRewards, Milesbar.com, MileSpree, Milesource.com, MyPoints.com, Silverclicks, SmartMile and WebMiles.com.

Most fell by the wayside when the dot-com bubble burst in 2000. Those that remain, such as ClickRewards.com and MyPoints.com, are shadows of their former selves. Travel rewards programs linked to bank-issued credit cards, by contrast, are currently in growth mode.

All major banks have their own offerings, which are independent of the airline programs: Bank of America's MilesEdge Visa, Bank One's Travel Plus Visa, Chase's Travel Rewards MasterCard, MBNA's WorldPoints Visa and so on.

In late 2004, Citibank (which also issues program specific cards for American Airlines and Hilton Hotels) launched its own entry, the PremierPass MasterCard.

Because miles earned for using these cards are proprietary—for example, they cannot be combined with miles from other programs—they generally have not found much favor with travelers who tend to use affinity credit cards associated with their chosen airline or hotel program.

Enroll: The Electronic Edge

As in other areas of operations, the airlines (and to a lesser extent the hotel chains) have been slowly but steadily moving many customer transactions onto their Web sites.

JetBlue's program, TrueBlue, is entirely online. No physical membership card; no paper account statements or newsletters. While other programs retain offline as well as online components, the trend is clearly in the direction of Web-based programs.

And that online functionality begins with signing up for the programs. Every program of any significance allows new members to enroll online. Elsewhere in this book, we have listed Web site addresses for most of the North American programs (on page 183).

And for those who have yet to embrace Web-based technology, yes, you can sign up by phone. You will find contact numbers on page 183 as well.

⊕ **REMEMBER THIS:**

- There is no single "best" program. (If there were, everyone would join that program and no others.)

- Join the program that allows you to earn the most awards and perks, with the least hassle.

- To earn the most awards, and maximize the chances of reaching elite status, concentrate mileage earning in as few programs as possible.

Chapter 4

The Art of Earning

IN THE WORLD OF MILES and points, earning is the name of the game. At one time, racking up frequent flyer miles was fairly simple: You signed up, boarded a plane, and flew. Then, after 25,000 miles or so, you had earned an award.

Things have changed.

Today, more than 50 percent of all miles and points are earned without ever leaving the ground. You can boost your account with co-branded affinity credit cards, telephone services, hotel stays, car rentals, restaurants, flowers, you name it. When you figure out how to use all of these mileage earning partners, your mileage score will skyrocket.

In the Cards

All major frequent travel programs have either teamed up with a bank to offer their own co-branded affinity credit card, or they have formed a partnership with Diners Club Club Rewards or American Express Membership Rewards. Credit cards let you earn miles or points for all purchases or charges. Earning power and benefits vary depending on the frequent travel program, your status in that program and the card you choose, whether it is Classic, Gold, Silver or Platinum.

If you charge your rent, gasoline, groceries, clothing, sundries, medical bills, business expenses, travel, utilities, tuition, car repair, phone calls, charitable contributions and gifts to a credit card, you may be rewarded each year with one or two free coach tickets. Add to the total miles earned through partners and actual flights and you could earn enough miles to take your family on a free vacation. If these tickets are used for destinations that normally cost a bundle, using a co-branded affinity credit card is a real payoff.

Real Estate/Mortgages

Time to talk about how to win by being on the "home" team. Your house (or, for that matter, any piece of real estate) can be one of the most valuable assets you possess when it comes to earning miles. If you plan to refinance, sell or buy a home, check your airline program's list of real estate partners that will reward you with miles. Since transactions are big, so are the amounts of miles you can earn.

Consider this: Buy a home for $300,000 and earn 90,000 bonus miles, enough for two free tickets to Hawaii with miles left over. How fast can you pack?

These offers can be broken out into several categories: Earning miles for listing your house for sale, earning miles for a "refi" or new mortgage, and even earning miles for the move itself.

Tip: It is not just airlines that are playing the real estate game. Check out your hotel programs and even your credit card programs for more ways to earn. American Express Membership Rewards members can earn 2,500 bonus points for every $10,000 of their home's value when selling it and Hilton HHonors members can earn 3,250 bonus points for every $10,000 when they refinance a home purchase.

Financial Services

Money may not buy happiness but it can earn miles. If you prefer to advance in the game of miles by investing there are plenty of ways to watch your miles grow. Investments, mutual funds and trading stocks can all cause your mileage earnings to increase in more ways than one. American Beacon Funds and Ameritrade are two familiar names.

For example, members of the America West Flight Fund program can earn up to 25,000 bonus miles when opening up a trading account with Ameritrade. American AAdvantage members can earn bonus miles with American Beacon Funds at an annualized rate of one mile for every $10.00 maintained in no-load, open-end mutual funds.

Telecommunications

MCI got the ball rolling for the telecommunications industry when it partnered with Northwest's WorldPerks program in 1987 offering five frequent flyer miles for each dollar spent on residential long distance. Since that time, every major frequent flyer program has offered miles for telephone usage. At one time most hotel programs offered similar deals, but those days are gone with the changing landscape of the telecommunications industry. No doubt this happened because of the hefty bonus offers program members earned. With the remaining telephone partners, a minimum must be spent on telephone services each month to accrue miles, and there is also a small tax on the miles earned.

Today's offers include long distance, cell phone and wireless plans. Other smaller offers include cell phone rental, calling cards and teleconferencing.

The standard bonus AT&T offers is 5,000 miles during a five-month period for residential long distance and an additional 5,000 bonus miles during a five-month period for AT&T Local Service. At the time this book was published, AT&T had cancelled their telephone partnerships with all major airlines except Continental OnePass.

Special note: As a general rule, do not sign up for local service or an unlimited service plan at the time you sign up for long distance service. You can usually get more miles by waiting until you are a customer before adding these services.

The recent merger of Nextel and Sprint will likely bring some mileage offer changes, but we do not believe it means the end of the almighty bonus mile. Sprint regularly offers 5,000 to 10,000 miles with various airlines for switching to their phone service. Airline Web sites offer links to standard deals.

However, better telecommunications deals do exist, and if you use the various resources listed at the end of this book, we can almost guarantee you will find information that can increase the number of bonus miles for which you might be eligible. Also, always ask about other possible bonuses for paying with an affinity credit card or for paying your bill online.

There is a trend requiring a $3.95 or higher telephone bill

MEMORABLE MOMENTS OF MILES & POINTS

JANUARY 1988

Delta Frequent Flyer announced that members could earn triple miles throughout 1988 when charging airline tickets with an American Express card. Other airlines quickly matched, but allowed the use of any credit card to purchase tickets and earn the bonus. Soon members of every major program were earning triple miles for all their flights during the entire year. This promotion is still the most important change in the industry because it demonstrated that these programs really worked. In the short time Delta and American Express offered triple miles, bookings at other airlines fell off.

per month to be eligible to earn miles at the standard five miles per dollar rate, so ask up front to avoid any surprises.

Because of the changes to airline telephone partners over the years, the current strategy is to use these services as "top off" or "secondary" programs. For instance, you may find that the 10,000-mile bonus (if available to you) is a cost effective way to top off one of your frequent flyer programs rather than buying the additional miles needed for a free ticket.

We are keen on the strategy of using telecommunications partners for secondary accounts since it is far too easy to end up with too many miles in a single account.

Frontier Airlines is an excellent example of a secondary account. If Frontier serves your city, the airline might be worth considering since their domestic awards are only 15,000 miles anywhere on their system. Their telecommunications partner is Qwest. A member can earn 5,000 bonus miles for using Qwest DSL service, another 2,000 bonus miles for Qwest long distance service and a bonus of 2,000 miles for choosing two products such as Quest Wireless and Quest Select Long Distance.

That is a total of 9,000 miles, which is a great deal considering their domestic award is only 15,000 miles. The same is true for members of the Alaska Mileage Plan living in Alaska where GCI is the partner. In this remote state, even cable TV earns you miles: Up to 10,000 bonus miles for new customer accounts and up to 500 bonus miles every six months.

In all these situations, pay your bills using your airline or hotel affinity credit card to leverage additional miles or points. Do not be afraid of the plastic fantastic.

Hotel and Car Rentals

Unlike many sports teams, your chances of doing well when you are on the road are pretty good when you are a frequent traveler. All you need is a little strategy. Pick hotels and car rental agencies that partner with your frequent flyer program and read all of the fine print. If you truly want to be a "mileage master" then "double dip" at every opportunity. Double dippers cleverly earn both airline miles and hotel points for the same stay.

Of course, you have to carefully plan your hotel stays and car rentals to be in conjunction with your flights and you must pay the eligible rates. If you want to go over the edge and become a "mileage junkie" (the equivalent of an Olympic athlete in the frequent flyer world) you can figure out how to stay at different partner hotels and rent from a different car rental company every day of your trip. An extra 500 miles per stay or car rental means 5,000 miles if you play musical hotel rooms or cars as opposed to 1,000 miles if you stay put. You will have to put up with a little packing and hassle, but, hey, no pain, no gain (or at least not quite as much gain). Note: Car rental earnings generally start at 50 miles per day.

Dining

The next time you are dining out alone or as host to dozens of people and you utter those infamous words "check, please," you might as well be ordering "more miles" from the menu. Dining programs offer a substantial number of bonus miles or points at more than 10,000 restaurants in the United States and Canada. Nine major frequent flyer programs (including American AAdvantage, British Airways Executive Club, Continental OnePass and Delta SkyMiles), as well as one hotel program (Priority Club Rewards) offer dining programs, which are coordinated by Rewards Network (formerly Transmedia and iDine). Rewards Network has three elite levels that offer increased earnings: Elite, Engaged and Active. Each level is attached to corresponding earning abilities, bonus opportunities and a roster of restaurants.

- Elite members who dine 12 or more times per calendar year will receive five miles for every dollar spent. These program members boast the greatest number of restaurants from which to choose and also enjoy a double bonus until June 30, 2006 allowing them to earn a total of 10 miles per dollar spent at all restaurants where benefits are offered.

- Engaged members receive three miles per dollar spent by creating an online user profile or by dining at least four times per calendar year at participating restaurants. This membership tier offers more restaurants and more bonus opportunities than the standard Active member.

- Active members are those who dine at least once per calendar year and who have not created an online user profile on the applicable airline dining program

Web site. Active members receive one mile per dollar spent at participating restaurants for their first three dines (during a single calendar year) and then earn three miles per dollar spent. They also qualify for periodic bonuses.

Priority Club members can earn up to 16 points per dollar spent. Membership in Rewards Network is free. (You can sign up online at www.rewardsnetwork.com.) Members who dine at participating restaurants will continue to receive miles based on the entire restaurant bill (including the cost of the meal, drinks, tip and taxes) when charged to a credit or debit card registered with Rewards Network.

Some airlines have their own unique list of dining partners. With Hawaiian Airlines, members can dine with dozens of restaurants in Hawaii and earn five to 10 miles per dollar spent on Visa or MasterCard. Members who have the Hawaiian Airlines Visa card can earn five additional bonus miles.

Shopping

Within the past two years there has been an explosion of "mileage malls" offered by airline and hotel loyalty programs.

Ever since it first occurred to a savvy retailer that frequent flyer miles could be used to grab a buyer's attention and spur increased sales, the airlines' mileage programs have been morphing gradually from frequent flyer programs into frequent buyer programs.

An online mileage mall (such as Northwest Airlines' online emporium, the WorldPerks Mall, which features more than 120 online merchants, from Apple Computers to VitaminShoppe.com) is a network of online merchants, all offering miles for shopping in the loyalty program of a particular airline. Generally, program members earn between one and 10 miles for every dollar spent at participating retailers.

Since the price is the same whether or not a buyer elects to earn miles, the mileage bonus truly represents added value. To put it differently, since there is no extra cost required to earn miles, the same item purchased from the same merchant without earning miles is effectively overpriced.

Like their bricks-and-mortar counterparts, online malls aim to lure shoppers with the promise of one-stop shopping. That means matching up a wide ranging roster of retailers offering products of every type and price range.

Tip: Some merchants, like Best Buy, allow you to order the product from the mileage mall to earn the miles, and then the option to pick up the item at the store just as you normally would. We bought a camera online, earned the miles, and then picked up the product at the store, all within an hour. That means a double dose of instant gratification.

For example, American Airlines' online emporium, the AAdvantage eShopping mall, features more than 90 online merchants, from Adidas.com to Wine.com. Other airline malls boast similarly robust merchant lineups.

All the Rest

If you decide to earn miles marathon style, it might go something like this: Buy flowers, shop on the Internet, subscribe to a magazine; the list continues. You could plan a day full of activities and purchases, each of which earns miles.

You may ask yourself where all these miles and points are coming from. In 1994, a whole new world of frequent flyer miles was created when American Airlines and United Airlines began selling miles to merchants who wanted to give customers a reward for loyalty. Now there are miles to be earned for doing everyday things and making everyday purchases. This marketing idea has expanded into an amazing opportunity to earn frequent flyer miles. So, whether you buy flowers from The Flower Club, eat dinner at your choice of thousands of participating restaurants, invest in a mutual fund, subscribe to some of your favorite magazines, or test drive a car, you can earn bonus miles in ways you never thought possible.

While these offers change almost daily, we have seen miles being offered for using an ATM, purchasing a heat pump, getting your hair cut, buying a condo in Las Vegas, and even buying chocolate pudding.

Another way to earn miles is on the Internet. There is no shortage of opportunities to earn miles and points for completing a survey online and—you guessed it—even for having online access itself.

As loyalty programs get more creative and the competition from low cost carriers continues, even better deals will be offered. Whatever your pleasure, you can probably earn thousands of miles by participating in such fun activities as reading, shopping, traveling, eating, driving and golfing. The possibilities are endless.

⊕ REMEMBER THIS:

- Did you know that American AAdvantage members can earn bonus miles with American Beacon Funds in this no-load, open-end mutual fund?

- Because of changes to airline telephone partners over the years, the best strategy is to use these services as "top off" or "secondary" programs.

- The fastest growing way to earn miles is with an online mileage mall: a network of online merchants all offering bonus miles for shopping.

Chapter 5

Plastic Magic: Credit Card Miles and Points

MILEAGE EARNING CREDIT CARDS HAVE been fixtures on the travel rewards scene since the mid 1980s, but the landscape has never been as cluttered as it is today. Cards of every imaginable type are competing for a place in consumers' wallets. The end result is a steady increase in card benefits.

Just the sheer number of cards—all with their distinct affiliations, fees and benefits—can drive would-be mileage accumulators to distraction. The cards break down neatly into three well-defined categories: Co-branded airline and hotel cards, multi-program, cards and bank cards with their own travel rewards programs. Each category has its own benefits and drawbacks, as explained in this chapter.

Airline/Hotel Co-branded Cards

Co-branded airline and hotel cards constitute the largest category and are used by the greatest number of frequent travelers. Each card is linked to a specific airline or hotel loyalty program. Typically, the cardholder earns one airline mile or hotel point for every dollar charged, plus a bonus for charging airline tickets on the host airline, or for charging stays at hotels associated with the hotel's loyalty program.

Familiar examples are the AAdvantage MasterCard, issued by Citibank; the Delta SkyMiles credit card, issued by American Express; and the Marriott Rewards Visa, issued by Chase.

Airline Specific Cards

These cards are generally referred to as airline affinity credit cards (because of the users' affinity with a particular airline) or co-branded cards (because the cards feature the logos of both the bank issuer and the airline hosting the loyalty program).

Costs

Annual fees range from $39 to $140 for credit cards associated with major airline programs, with many falling in the $45 to $65 range. The majority currently charges a 15.99 percent annual percentage rate (variable, Prime + 9.99 percent) on outstanding balances.

Mileage Earning Rate

As previously mentioned, the industry standard earning rate for airline affiliated credit cards is one mile for every dollar charged to the card. Assuming miles have a value of one to two cents each that amounts to a one to two percent rebate. The rebate is higher when cards are used to charge airline tickets on the airline hosting the credit card program since those purchases normally earn double miles.

Predictably, given the competitive pressure to capture the business of frequent travelers, perks are constantly being increased, both on a long term and on a promotional basis. The Delta SkyMiles card, for example, boasts "Always Double Miles"—double miles at qualifying stand alone supermarkets, drugstores, gas stations, home improvement and hardware stores, as well as the U.S. Postal Service. Following Delta down that same road, Continental's MasterCard from Chase also offers double miles for charges at selected merchants.

And on a limited time basis, the card issuers are ratcheting up the number of miles new cardholders receive after their first charge, such as 15,000 on the AAdvantage MasterCard.

Perhaps the most significant development in the benefits area has been the awarding of elite qualifying miles for card use. There have been a number of recent promotions awarding elite miles for non-flight activities. But the boldest move yet in decoupling elite qualification from actually flying is United's latest Mileage Plus Platinum Visa, which allows cardholders to earn up to 15,000 elite qualifying miles annually for charges. (Mileage Plus Classic and Gold Visa cards also have awarded up to 5,000 elite qualifying miles, but only on a limited time promotional basis.)

Annual Earning Cap

Although it is a moot point for most consumers, many cards impose an annual cap on mileage earning, generally ranging between 50,000 and 100,000 miles. The limit typically is raised or waived altogether for cards with higher annual fees and for elite members.

As an example, the annual maximum is 60,000 miles for the regular United Mileage Plus Visa card ($60 annual fee) and 100,000 for the Gold card ($85 annual fee), but there is no mileage cap for Mileage Plus Premier, Premier Executive or Premier Executive 1K members. And with United's highest priced card, the Mileage Plus Platinum Visa ($140 annual fee), no annual cap is imposed regardless of a member's tier status.

Business Cards

It is worth noting that many of the same credit card issuers offering airline affiliated cards to individuals also offer airline affiliated mileage cards to businesses.

Designed specifically for smaller businesses, the cards are enhanced with benefits such as periodic account summaries, discounted business services and higher annual mileage earning limits.

Business cards are issued in the names of those employees authorized to charge goods and services in the course of conducting company business. Their miles are earned into the account of a designated individual—generally the business owner—who can then choose to use the miles either for his or her personal use or to offset the cost of future company business travel.

Debit Cards

Also worth mentioning under the heading of airline affinity credit cards are airline debit cards, also called check cards or ATM cards.

Larger programs typically offer a choice between a debit card with a lower annual fee that awards only one-half mile per dollar spent and a card with a higher annual fee that awards a full mile for every dollar spent.

As an example, for $30 a year, the Continental Airlines Banking Card from Chase can be linked to a regular Chase checking account and earn one OnePass mile for every $2 spent; or for $65 a year, OnePass members can link a Continental Banking Card to an upgraded Chase Select Checking account, which earns a more generous one mile per dollar.

Because debit cards are directly linked to a checking account, they require the cardholder to maintain a checking account with the same bank that issues the card. That can be a deal breaker for those who have a pre-existing relationship with a local bank they wish to preserve.

Hotel Specific Cards

As with hotel programs in general, hotel affiliated credit cards suffer an inferiority complex compared to cards linked to airline programs. This is unwarranted since, as airline ticket prices have fallen and hotel rates have risen, the value of hotel points and awards has increased significantly compared to airline program awards. Still, when it comes time to pay the bill, travelers are much more likely to reach for an airline card than a hotel card.

That competitive disadvantage has spurred hotel card issuers to try harder, offering more benefits and lower costs. Where airline cards charge significant annual fees, their hotel counterparts are typically available for no annual fee. And if an annual fee is imposed, that fee will likely be waived for the first year.

In another benefits category, where the airlines have just begun awarding elite qualifying miles for charges, several of the hotel cards already have a long history of granting elite status outright to new cardholders, either as limited time offers or, in the case of Marriott's card, as a permanent card feature.

Costs

As already mentioned, there are no annual fees for most hotel cards. And while the credit cards for Marriott and Starwood programs have $30 annual fees, they are waived for the first year.

As with the airline cards, the annual percentage rates for most hotel cards is currently 15.99 percent (variable, Prime + 9.99 percent).

Earning Rates

Hotel cards award one or more points for every dollar spent on purchases charged to them, and usually supplement the normal earning rate with a bonus when the card is used to charge hotel stays.

The Hilton HHonors Platinum card, for instance, awards users with five HHonors points when charging stays at Hilton Family hotels, and three points for other charges. On the other hand, Marriott Rewards Visa cardholders

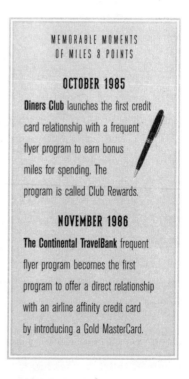

MEMORABLE MOMENTS
OF MILES 8 POINTS

OCTOBER 1985

Diners Club launches the first credit card relationship with a frequent flyer program to earn bonus miles for spending. The program is called Club Rewards.

NOVEMBER 1986

The Continental TravelBank frequent flyer program becomes the first program to offer a direct relationship with an airline affinity credit card by introducing a Gold MasterCard.

earn three points for charges at hotels in the Marriott network, and one point for non-hotel charges.

Because earning and redemption rates in competing hotel programs tend to be fundamentally different, it is difficult to make apples-to-apples comparisons. When comparing hotel programs, and their associated credit cards, it is not the absolute number of points earned for a given transaction that gives it the most credence. Rather, it is how far those points go toward qualifying for an award. For instance, Starwood's Preferred Guest program awards two Starpoints for every dollar spent at Starwood hotels, and offers free weekend nights for as few as 2,000 points. Marriott's Rewards program awards 10 points per dollar spent at most Marriott brands and charges 7,500 points for a free weekend night. Using these two examples, Marriott Rewards is the faster way to a free weekend night.

Multi-Program Cards

What we are calling multi-program (or multi-currency) cards are the American Express Preferred Rewards card linked to its Membership Rewards program and the Diners Club card linked to the Club Rewards program.

For frequent travelers, the key benefit of these cards is that points earned for using the cards can be exchanged for miles and points in the programs of multiple participating airlines and hotels.

Costs

The annual fees for entry level American Express and Diners cards are $110 and $95 per year respectively. These fees are significantly higher than the fees attached to the majority of airline and hotel rewards cards. These fees are higher because both credit cards tend to provide more benefits than other cards; for instance, the Diners Club card provides primary rather than secondary car insurance coverage when renting a car, thus allowing you the ability to save money.

Since these are charge cards—not credit cards—the balance must be completely paid off each month. Consequently, there is no annual percentage rate because there are no outstanding balances.

Also in contrast to airline cards, there are fees when redeeming points for airline miles.

In 2002, Diners began imposing a "handling fee" of 95 cents to redeem Club Rewards points for 1,000 frequent flyer miles. So, to redeem enough points for a 25,000-mile free domestic coach ticket, the fee would be $23.75.

In the spirit of besting the competition, when American Express instituted its own redemption fee for airline miles, it chose to undercut Diners Club, charging 40 cents per 1,000 miles redeemed, with a maximum fee of $50. Another point in favor of the American Express policy: A fee is only assessed when cardholders redeem for miles in a U.S. program and not for an international program as the fee is tied to the Federal Excise Tax for miles purchased from a U.S. airline program.

Earning Rate
Both cards award one point for every dollar charged. But, with the "Always Double Miles" feature, American Express cardholders earn two Membership Rewards points for every dollar purchased with the card at qualifying stand-alone supermarkets, drugstores, gas stations, home improvement stores, the U.S. Postal Service and for payments to your wireless phone bill. (Examples of merchants include: Safeway, Krogers, Walgreens, Amoco, The Home Depot, Lowe's, Nextel and Verizon.)

Partnerships

In most participating airline programs, American Express and Diners Club points exchange at a one-to-one ratio.

American Express allows Membership Rewards points to be converted into the programs of 11 airlines and four hotels:

- *Airlines* — AeroMexico, All Nippon, Continental, Delta, El Al, GlobalPass, Hawaiian, JetBlue, Mexicana, Southwest, US Airways and Virgin

- *Hotels* — Best Western, Hilton, Priority Club and Starwood

Conspicuously missing from the Membership Rewards partner roster are three of the largest U.S. airline programs: American AAdvantage, Northwest WorldPerks and United Mileage Plus.

Diners Club points are exchangeable into 25 airline and seven hotel programs as follows:

- *Airlines* — Air Canada, Air France, Alaska Airlines, America West, American, Asiana, British Airways, Continental, Delta, El Al, Frontier, Hawaiian, GlobalPass, Iceland Air, Korean, Mexicana, Midwest, Northwest, SAS, South African Air, Southwest, Thai, United, US Airways and Virgin

- *Hotels* — Best Western, Choice, Hilton, Hyatt, Marriott, Priority Club and Starwood

Bank Travel Rewards Cards

The latest development in the miles-for-charges arena is credit cards with a travel rewards component now offered by most major card issuers. (Note: These cards are not affiliated with a specific airline loyalty program.) Prominent among them: The MilesEdge

Visa from Bank of America, the TravelPlus Visa from BankOne, the Go Miles Visa from Capital One, the Travel Rewards Master-Card from Chase and the PremierPass MasterCard from Citibank.

These are MasterCard or Visa cards that reward users with "miles" or points for charges just as the credit cards linked to airline and hotel programs do. And on the award side, the miles can be redeemed for free flights just as they can be with airline programs.

Indeed, these bank programs were designed to shamelessly mimic the airline programs in the hope of duplicating their considerable success. But because miles and points earned with a bank card cannot be put into an airline or hotel loyalty program, travelers who elect to participate in a traditional airline or hotel program and a bank card program will find themselves with two separate, non-combinable types of miles and points.

For travelers content with earning miles solely via their credit card purchases, bank cards can be decidedly superior to airline

Summary of Travel Rewards Cards		
	Airline Cards	Hotel Cards
Fees	Medium	Low-Medium
Strengths	Miles combinable with miles from other program partners (airlines, hotels, etc.) to quickly reach award thresholds such as free flights and elite status	• Low cost • Award stays are readily available (and worth more as hotel rates have increased relative to airfares)
Weaknesses	• Earning and redemption limited to a single program • Blackout dates and capacity controls limit award availability	Hotel programs generally play smaller parts in earning awards, so points have less value in the sense of less purpose because people are more focused on miles than on hotel points and airline programs
Recommended Role	Primary card for frequent flyers who concentrate activity in a single airline program	Secondary card for frequent flyers, to add free hotel nights to free flights from airline programs

loyalty programs when redeeming miles. Where airline program awards are notoriously and sometimes maddeningly restricted, free tickets earned from bank card miles are readily available with no blackout dates. That is because when a bank card member redeems miles, the bank simply purchases a ticket in the marketplace on the member's behalf. And that ticket can be on most any airline, not just on a short list of preferred partners. (Note: Bank card programs are not affiliated with any hotels.)

Costs

Among bank cards' most attractive features are their low costs. Annual fees for the cards range from zero to $39.

Annual percentage rates are on the low side as well; generally several percentage points below the rates charged for airline cards.

Earning

Like their airline program counterparts, bank cards typically

Summary of Travel Rewards Cards		
	Multi-Program Cards	Bank Cards
Fees	Medium	Low-Medium
Strengths	• Flexibility to convert points to miles in selected airline and hotel programs • Wide choice of awards • Points don't expire	• Low costs • No blackout dates on award travel • Wide choice of airlines for award travel
Weaknesses	• High annual fees • Fees to convert points to airline miles; no fees for hotel points • Amex points cannot be converted to American or United miles	• Cannot be combined with airline miles • Award tickets require 21-day advance booking and cannot exceed a set dollar value • Miles expire
Recommended Role	• Primary card for frequent travelers who must participate in multiple airline programs • Secondary card for frequent flyers who participate in multiple hotel programs	Primary card for consumers who earn the bulk of their miles by using a credit card

award one mile or point for every dollar in net purchases charged to the card.

Unlike airline miles, miles in most bank card programs have limited life spans, typically expiring after three to five years. Miles in major airline programs can be extended indefinitely with a single account transaction every 36 months.

While this will not matter to most consumers, know that there is generally a limit to the number of miles that may be earned monthly and/or annually with bank cards.

Awards

In keeping with their self conscious cloning of airline programs, bank cards have priced their awards at levels similar to airline programs. For a coach ticket within the contiguous United States, 25,000 to 35,000 bank miles are the norm.

On the upside, bank card awards are not restricted. If a seat is available that meets the advance purchase time and price criteria, the member may claim it. Reminder: There are no blackout dates.

Another significant plus over airline program awards: The bank card award ticket may be issued for travel on just about any major airline.

On the negative side, award tickets must be requested at least 21 days in advance and a Saturday-night stay is generally required. And the dollar value of the award ticket is capped. For a free U.S. domestic coach award, the maximum value is between $300 and $500, depending on the bank card program.

(A new wrinkle in award pricing comes from Capital One's latest Go Miles card. Miles required for an award ticket are computed by multiplying the lowest available fare by 90. So, an award ticket that could be purchased for $300 would cost 27,000 miles.)

Summary: Choice Points

As with airline and hotel programs, there is no single credit, charge or bank card that best meets the needs of everyone who aspires to earn free travel. (It should be stressed that the decision to pursue travel rewards is ultimately an emotional one. For those with different priorities, there are other cards that generate cash rebates or discounts toward the purchase of a car, or any number of other rewards or rebates.)

At the end of the day, the best cards are those that conform to your lifestyle on two key fronts: First, are you principally a frequent flyer or frequent buyer (or somewhere in between)? And secondly, if you are frequent flyers, can you confine yourself to a single card? Because fees are associated with these cards, there is an even more compelling reason for you to stay confined to a single card, possibly with a second card playing a supporting role.

For those who earn a significant number of miles by actually traveling, the choice of a credit card should simply follow and complement the choice of an airline program. In other words, use the card affiliated with your primary airline program.

A hotel program's credit card can be used to supplement earnings from an airline card by accruing sufficient points to obtain free hotel nights that can complement free flights earned from an airline program.

Frequent travelers who cannot consolidate their earnings in a single program—because of, say, a company travel policy—should stick to multi-program cards such as American Express Membership Rewards and Diners Club Club Rewards. These cards function as primary cards, provided their participating airlines are the ones you are flying. Multi-program cards can also be used as secondary cards in place of a hotel card.

While considerations of cost and account management argue against maintaining too many active credit cards, multiple cards judiciously chosen and used can be used to good effect.

For example, secondary cards can extend the life of miles in less active accounts and they can be used to top off accounts when an award threshold is within reach. An American Express or Diners Club card can be handy in that regard. But one of the hotel affiliated cards, several of which have no annual fee, may be a more cost effective solution. Use the hotel card to earn points, which can be transferred for no fee as needed into participating airline programs. (For information on points-to-miles conversion rates go to the Converting Miles and Points into Money chapter on page 136.)

If you do opt for a second or third card, bear in mind the benefits of brand diversification. Oftentimes, mileage or points promotions will be targeted to users of a Visa, MasterCard or American Express card. So, having multiple credit cards can translate into expanded earning opportunities.

As a side note: In this period of financial instability in the travel industry, multi-program cards offer consumers a welcome modicum of safety and stability. Unlike the airlines, both American Express and Diners (a subsidiary of mighty Citibank) are in tip-top financial shape. So, while miles earned directly in an airline program may be at risk of the airline liquidating its assets and voiding the miles in its loyalty program, points retained in the programs of American Express and Diners Club enjoy a kind of safe harbor existence.

For infrequent flyers who plan on earning the bulk of their miles through credit card use, bank cards offer a cost effective way of earning the occasional free flight, without the hassle and anxiety associated with capacity controlled awards in the airlines' own programs.

Finally, if elite perks are a priority, the choice is limited to a card linked directly to the airline or hotel program.

Obviously, there is no chance of attaining elite status by racking up miles with bank cards since they are independent of airline and hotel programs.

When to Pass on Plastic

As with any activity that potentially earns miles, consumers should beware of overpaying for the privilege.

To use real world numbers, if a card has an annual fee of $50 and the prospective cardholder expects to incur finance charges of another $50 over the course of a year, it is only reasonable to expect to earn enough miles to at least offset that $100 expense. Assuming each mile is worth two cents (which is generous) the cardholder would need to earn 5,000 miles in 12 months to cover the costs associated with the card. Since most cards award one mile for every dollar charged, that amounts to charging $5,000 a year, or about $417 per month. If the assumed value of a mile is reduced to one cent, your spending target doubles to $10,000.

⊕ REMEMBER THIS:

- ◈ After flight miles, using a program affiliated credit card is the most popular source of frequent flyer miles.

- ◈ Frequent flyers should first choose an airline program, and then sign up for the credit card linked to that program.

- ◈ Frequent buyers can earn free trips without the high fees of airline affiliated credit cards by participating in a bank card's travel rewards program.

Chapter 6

Cashing In: How to Redeem Your Miles

AS WE HAVE WRITTEN, EARNING miles is easy these days but redeeming them for awards can be difficult.

Here is a simple, if hard-to-believe fact: On any given day, 100 percent of airline seats are available for award redemption.

We thought that would catch your attention.

One hundred percent? Then how come you are rarely awarded one?

To understand award redemption we need to take a step back to 1981. When frequent flyer programs were invented, every seat on the aircraft was available to members each and every day. No blackout dates or capacity controls existed. The price? Awards were set at 40,000 to 50,000 miles for a seat in coach class.

By 1988, concern that the number of outstanding frequent flyer miles could eventually become a problem for the airline industry was a real reason to re-evaluate. United Mileage Plus began to let miles expire after a certain period of time. Members were not exactly thrilled with the idea, so to ease the pain, programs began to offer new awards at lower levels that at the time started at 20,000 miles. These lower level awards came with restrictions limiting the number of free seats per flight.

Members clamored to take advantage of these new, lower cost awards that were adjusted in the 1990s to an industry standard of 25,000 miles. Today, nearly 83 percent of all awards are at the lower, more restricted award level. Nonetheless, the fact remains that 100 percent of airline seats daily are available for award redemption at the original, higher level (40,000 to 50,000 miles)—a category often referred to as "any time" awards.

MEMORABLE MOMENTS
OF MILES & POINTS

JULY 1988

United Mileage Plus introduces capacity controls and blackout dates to its frequent flyer program; other airlines quickly followed.

The past few years have been particularly difficult for the redemption of frequent flyer awards. Because a number of airlines are in and out of bankruptcy, and because the possibility of labor strikes and mergers is so real, a significant number of award redemptions maintain "ghost" itineraries. That is, people are redeeming awards solely to protect miles should an airline liquidate. For instance, during the past two years, many members of the US Airways Dividend Miles program redeemed their miles on partner United Airlines, fearing that US Airways was not going to make it. Of course, this made it even more difficult for members of United's program to redeem their miles. In this case, US Airways members were booking only temporary awards, hoping to redeposit their miles upon news that US Airways would survive.

Even in the best of times, many frequent flyers report that they are not able to redeem award tickets. This is especially true for elite-level members who have followed all the correct procedures. Even the Delta SkyMiles membership guide specifically states: "Seats available for Award Travel are limited and may not be available on all flights."

It seems that airlines are making the effort to structure their award redemption processes with less mystery and difficulty, although many frequent flyers consider these efforts to be too little, too late.

There are a few important issues that as a frequent flyer, you should be aware of. These factors could affect how and when you use your miles.

Blackout dates (restricted travel dates), peak travel periods, origination points and length-of-stay restrictions can be formidable obstacles. Since all programs have different policies, procedures and technologies for securing award travel, the entire process can be overwhelming. Tighter seating restrictions

MEMORABLE MOMENTS
OF MILES & POINTS

MARCH 1989

In response to an increase in the number of miles required to receive some of United's more popular awards, **outraged Mileage Plus members filed a class action lawsuit,** represented by two Chicago law firms. Cook County Circuit Judge Arthur L. Dunn ruled in favor of the plaintiffs and United revised its Mileage Plus program allowing members who had accumulated miles under the old system more time to use those miles under the prior award structure.

because of the rise in travel, additional fees and changing program rules are just a few of the hurdles you may have to face. Below are some common restrictions that accompany programs.

- *Increased miles:* Since 2001, most airlines have raised the mileage requirements of select awards or upgrades. Most often these have been in the premium class awards such as business and international first class, and for upgrades when used with a lower cost coach ticket.

- *Extra fees:* It is not free travel if you are required to pay additional money. If you change the date or time of your flight, you may be charged a fee. If you change your flight's destination, that could mean another fee. Want to cancel and use your mileage for something different? You guessed it—you could be charged a fee. Award tickets include the 9/11 Security Fee of up to $10 per roundtrip, as well as U.S. or foreign user, inspection, customs, security or other similar taxes, fees or charges of up to $250, depending on the itinerary.

- *Seating restrictions:* If you are hoping to plan a family vacation with your miles, make sure you are prepared to divide and conquer. On some flights, you may be limited to a maximum of two seats, meaning the family may have to fly on different planes and/or arrive at different times.

Bonus Tip: You should always keep your frequent flyer number handy when speaking with the airlines or booking online. You purchase a ticket with miles the same way you do with a credit card. They will use your number to access your account and subtract the necessary amount of miles. Tickets are rarely available in paper form, with airlines opting for electronic methods to book, redeem and deliver your free seats.

The following pointers will help flyers stay on the right track to award redemption.

- *Plan ahead.* Award seats are best booked ahead of time. Generally, flights are available for award booking 11 months in advance. Note: It could cost you if you need express reservations.

- *Understand upgrades.* Many programs have restrictions on using award miles to upgrade your ticket. To avoid frustration, ask before redeeming.

- *When planning your award travel, strive to make it worth every penny you spent earning all those miles.* Check airfares to your desired destinations before spending any miles. If you find the cost is low (less than $225), then do not use your miles for this trip. Save your miles for a more expensive ticket, or to purchase an upgrade.

- *Look at the big picture before spending your money.* It may behoove you to pay for vacation flights as they usually have high competition for award seats. Use your awards for flights that are less popular, particularly if those routes are shorter and do not earn many miles. Your mileage earning potential on long trips is obviously greater. Also, keep in mind that many airlines offer special deals on awards for short-haul trips. For instance, American and United both recently offered awards for flights less than 750 miles each way for only 15,000 miles.

- *Before you book your reservation, know how many miles are in your account then make sure all the miles or points you need are available, especially if you have to transfer them from one account to another.* Also, ensure that miles from all of your most recent trips are posted in your account. Not having enough miles when you book will definitely preclude you from getting a seat, even if you know the miles will be in your account soon.

◆ *Decide what you want to do and where you want to do it yet do not be too attached to your plans.* Choose several possible destinations, keeping in mind that popular destinations are often booked three to 11 months in advance.

◆ *After you have decided on several possible destinations, choose your travel dates with just as much flexibility.* Plan your vacation to begin and end midweek. Fridays and Saturdays are unfavorable days on which to start an award trip. Avoid flights close to holidays. By planning travel that avoids peak travel times, you can increase your chances of getting the travel award you want.

◆ *After trying—but not succeeding—to redeem your miles online, decide whether or not to book your award reservations through the service center, keeping in mind that Mondays and Fridays are high call volume days.* If your program's service center is open 24 hours a day, try calling at night or late in the afternoon on Tuesday, Wednesday or Thursday. Service center agents can assist you in rerouting an award through various city pairs, something an online system has not yet perfected.

- *Do not call a service center until you are ready to book. You may not get a second chance because many airlines will not hold a reservation for an award seat if you do not immediately book.* Do not let high demand seats slip away because you were not ready to commit.

- *Ask for suggestions from friends.* Instead of just talking about the latest bonus promotions, find out who is actually enjoying good luck in getting the seats they want and to which destinations they desire. Consider choosing places that are not tourist attractions. If a friend suggests a place you have never heard of, keep an open mind. Remember the adage: "The greatest adventure awaits those who have nothing planned."

- *If the flight you want is booked, try to waitlist and call back frequently to check your status.* A seat that is not available today can be yours tomorrow if you are persistent. Unsold seats on regular flights are opened up for award travel at the last moment.

- *If your program does not allow waitlisting, it is still worth your while to call back on a frequent basis.* Most awards are capacity controlled and, while there may not be a seat available today, someone may change plans tomorrow and you could get that reservation with a well-timed call.

- *Do not be too choosy with your departure and arrival times.* Flights scheduled for late at night and during the midmorning often have greater availability.

- *Try several routes to your desired destination.* Making connections through different airports may allow you more opportunity to arrange a seat. Also, try making your final destination a city that is close to where you really want to go. A nearby city may not have as much traffic and, therefore, may offer more available seats. For example, if you want to go to San Francisco, and the award seats are gone, try Oakland or San Jose. You can then drive the short distance to your actual destination. This applies to Europe as well. If London is your destination, it is easy to get there after landing in, say, Brussels or Dublin.

- *Look for flights that include stops.* Traditionally, nonstop flight availability is the first thing the reservation system searches out. Though stops require you to spend a few more hours in the air or a few more hours at an airport, you may have a layover that is long enough to allow you the luxury of checking out a new city.

- *When making award flight reservations, ask about stopover options.* A three-day stopover in Hawaii on your way to Bangkok could be just the ticket that will transform your award travel into the vacation of a lifetime. Some programs allow two stopovers, while some only allow stopovers for less than 24 hours.

- *Some programs allow members to opt for "open-jaw" award flights.* For example, you can depart from New York, fly to London, travel through Europe by train or car, and depart from Athens back to New York. Open-jaw tickets typically cost twice as much as normal tickets. Consequently, open-jaw award tickets can (but do no always) cost you more miles. In fact, because of the open-jaw flexibility you are more likely to get the award you want. Open-jaw tickets are flexible because you do not have to return from the city to which you flew. You can choose any other return city. It is similar to buying two one-way tickets rather than a single roundtrip.

♦ *Consider flying in first or business class.* Because they require fewer miles, coach awards are usually the first to go. By redeeming more miles for a business class or first class ticket, you will be pampered (OK, at least you will enjoy more legroom) and may have a better chance of getting an award.

♦ *Consider a vacation during the off-peak season, which typically is not during the summer.* Because of year-round schooling, there are more options these days to travel on awards than just during the months of June, July and August.

♦ *If you do not want to bother with blackout dates or capacity controls (which can limit your award choices) then spend more miles.* Although they usually require twice the miles, "any time" awards offered by all major airlines can assure you a seat when regular awards are hard to come by.

♦ *If your schedule is flexible, look into last-minute online award sales offered by programs such as American AAdvantage and Continental OnePass.* For a significant reduction in miles, you can take domestic and inter-national trips, but you will have to have your bags packed at all times.

▶ *Finding award seats becomes more difficult when you are traveling as a family. Singles and couples usually have the best chance of getting a free seat.* Your best bet is to get as many award seats as possible and then purchase the additional seats as needed. Remember, if you are traveling with family members who rarely fly, use the award ticket for your family member and purchase your own ticket. This way, you will be replenishing your account with the miles you earn from flying, while your family enjoys traveling for free. Plus, companion award tickets usually require less mileage than a normal award ticket does. A great example of a companion ticket using hotel points is Hilton HHonors. You can redeem 40,000 HHonors points for one companion coach ticket on United Airlines within the continental 48 United States and Canada with the purchase of a valid published fare with the same itinerary. By itself, one coach ticket within the continental 48 United States and Canada costs 100,000 HHonors points.

▶ *If you are not able to get an award with your airline, check out your hotel programs' point balances. Hotel programs such as Best Western, Hilton, Hyatt, Marriott and TripRewards offer flight awards, or a combination hotel and flight award packages.* The flight awards offered by hotels are often taken from a different inventory than award seats offered by the airlines. You may have much better luck getting your dream vacation if you go through a hotel program. This is because airlines will often hold extra award seats for

their program partners. Note: You will not lose miles
converting hotel points into airline miles. You can
lose miles when you go through a double conversion,
for example, hotel to airline to another airline, or
airline to hotel and back to another airline.

♦ *Go that extra mile for elite status.* Many programs
waive blackout dates and capacity controls (the two
biggest obstacles for getting an award ticket) for
certain elite-level flyers. Furthermore, with many
programs, booking agents are trained to respect your
status. It is well known that employees staffing the
elite-level desks at airlines are senior in rank and
often have many more years experience in making
reservations of any kind, whether that is free travel or
paid fare. Use that extra experience to your advantage.

Award Alternatives

Sometimes, despite your best efforts, a free trip is not always in
the cards. We suggest the following alternatives.

♦ *Do not get hung up on free airline travel.* We find that
many travelers make the mistake of assuming miles
should always be redeemed for airline tickets. Here
is something to consider: Many flyers complain about
not getting the free ticket they want due to capacity
controls yet they spend hundreds or thousands of
dollars on hotel rooms. Consider purchasing an
airline ticket and applying your miles to a hotel room.

Both American's and United's frequent flyer programs
allow their members to convert their miles into free

hotel stays. American allows all members to redeem miles for free nights at Marriott and InterContinental Hotels, while United only allows their 1K, Premier Executive and Premier members to have the benefit. For instance, you can redeem 4,000 Mileage Plus miles and get a voucher for $100 off a two-night stay at any U.S. Hyatt hotel.

- *Combine paid and award travel.* For example, you could pay to fly to Los Angeles or New York using a low cost carrier and then pay for the next leg of your trip with miles as you continue on to Hawaii or Europe. Or simply buy the extra miles you need. Many programs allow mileage purchases if you have accumulated close to the necessary amount for a free ticket.

- *View companion awards and upgrades as viable alternatives to free awards.* Each of these suggestions requires you to purchase a paid ticket from the airline, and airlines always want to sell a seat even if it costs them one; for example, when the companion is flying for free.

- *As strange as this might sound, unless you are an elite member of a program, consider switching to a program that has a better history of providing awards.* Among the programs that have the best award seat availability are Alaska Mileage Plan, Southwest Rapid Rewards and American AAdvantage.

Other Tips

- With Hilton and Marriott, know the award code you wish to use, and persuade the reservations agent to call

the hotel directly if award availability is gone. Sometimes exceptions will be made. Each reward available
through Marriott Rewards is assigned a unique reward
code. For example, the award code for seven free
nights split between any three Hawaiian hotels participating in the Marriott Rewards program is 563.

- Programs like Diners Club Club Rewards and American
  Express Membership Rewards offer the most flexibility
  to "put miles and points where you need them."
  American Express alone has 20 airline partners and
  more than 150 worldwide hotel properties as partners.

- Several hotel programs' all-inclusive awards that
  include air, hotel and even car rental are terrific
  because they offer several airlines from which to
  choose, and they can usually get the awards you
  want, regardless of the time of year.

- Short haul U.S. destinations —at least those that do
  not go through a hub connection—are always a good
  bet for a free ticket because the more flight segments
  your award has, the more problems you will incur in
  securing award availability.

- Elite members have much more freedom when booking
  awards. Airline and hotel programs often make more
  awards available to their elite members and in some
  situations even lift restrictions from blackout dates.
  These exceptions often make earning elite status that
  much more of a benefit.

The battle for more award seats on desirable flights will
likely be a heated one and one that will not soon be

resolved—given that travel is on the rebound and award flyers do have to share the same plane with paying customers. If the current trend continues to lower the cost of paying to fly, then these flights will certainly continue to be full. Until then, the best advice for getting the award you want is to use your head and be flexible. Remember to use your knowledge and consider all the angles before you start planning an award trip.

10 Best Ways to Redeem Your Miles

10. While the attention has always been on redeeming frequent flyer miles, we advise members of all programs to brush up on the value of hotel points. Hotel points have much more flexibility than airline miles based on the variety of "brands." For instance, if you have a problem redeeming hotel points with Marriott, inquire about other brands in the Marriott family such as Courtyard, Renaissance Hotel, Residence Inn or Fairfield Inn properties. Fact: We rarely hear complaints about hotel redemption. Also consider that these days hotel rates have been climbing while airline prices have been falling.

9. You have heard about planning early for frequent flyer award redemption. Now try this: Plan late. Airlines are getting better at releasing seats at the last minute for award redemption. Best time? Try two weeks before a scheduled flight. Even better is to know the airlines' "sweet spot" for seat inventory adjustment. In recent research, Continental's award availability was spotty at 330 days in advance, six months in advance, 30 days in advance, and even two weeks in advance. However, in the test, which involved 12 different city pairs for award redemption, awards were available at the three-month advance time frame 100 percent of the time. While this does not guarantee you will be so lucky, it does mean that Continental has a sweet spot.

8. Codeshare an award. With airline alliances, sometimes airlines only have half the plane to give away as awards since their codeshare partner owns the remaining seats. Because one airline will only see their available seats, try asking about their codeshare partner's free seats.

7. The family plan. Most people do not have enough miles for the whole family to fly for free and often purchase a ticket for one of the kids to go along on the vacation. Tip: Whenever you have to purchase a ticket along with an award, transfer your award to a family member and fly on the purchased ticket yourself. Why? You will replenish your miles plus you will qualify for selected benefits like upgrades when using a revenue ticket. Another trick for using miles for a family vacation is to use miles from one of your frequent flyer program's partners. Perhaps you can only get a single award seat using your SkyMiles on Delta. Try using your Continental or Northwest miles (either you have them or can redeem them from a credit card or hotel program) for other seats on the same Delta flight. (Remember: These airlines are part of the same airline alliance, SkyTeam.) Sometimes, each airline partner has a different award bucket and seat allocation for a particular flight.

6. Mini awards. Both American and Continental offer weekend awards to select cities for fewer miles than normal. Fly out late on Friday or Saturday, and return Sunday, Monday or Tuesday. While restrictions do apply, you can claim an award for as few as 7,500 miles. Nearly every member we spoke to did not even know these special award offers existed but they do! This is a great way for a savvy traveler to find awards at only 12,500 miles or even less.

5. Use your mileage pool. If you have been smart, in addition to your airline miles you also have points with American Express or Diners Club, or with hotel programs like Starwood Preferred Guest, Hilton HHonors or Priority Club Rewards. If so, take advantage of these programs' flexibilities and try award travel on an airline other than the one you normally fly. Remember: You can transfer points from all five of these programs into an existing or a new frequent flyer airline account for award redemption. Just because you have not flown with an airline does not mean you cannot redeem an award with them. Note: There is no loss of miles or points because we are only referring to a single redemption and not an "exchange" in which case points or miles would likely lose some value. An "exchange" is when hotel points are converted into miles via a middleman such as Amtrak Guest Rewards. (See chapter 8 for more information on exchanging miles and hotel points.)

4. Know the best days to travel. Best Days within the United States: Monday, Tuesday, Wednesday; to Florida: Monday, Tuesday, Wednesday; to Hawaii: Tuesday, Wednesday, Thursday; to Asia: Tuesday, Wednesday, Thursday; to the Caribbean: Tuesday, Wednesday; to Europe: Tuesday, Wednesday, Thursday; to Mexico: Tuesday, Wednesday; to South America: Tuesday, Wednesday. Worst Days within the United States: Friday,

Sunday; to Florida: Friday, Sunday; to Hawaii: Friday, Saturday, Sunday, Monday; to Asia: Friday, Saturday, Sunday; to the Caribbean: Saturday, Sunday, Monday; to Europe: Friday, Saturday, Sunday; to Mexico: Friday, Saturday, Sunday; to South America: Friday, Saturday, Sunday.

3. Go where no one else has gone (yet). The secret is to look for new routes opening up. Those seats have not yet been available for either ticket sales or award redemption, which means everything is available. This requires you to read travel news about an airline's new "second daily flight" or their newly released "winter schedule." *Frequent Flyer* magazine's Regions section (www.frequentflyer.oag.com) is a great source for new routes.

2. Book an award by segments. Because of the "hub and spoke" system that most major airlines use, the problem with getting a free ticket is not that the entire route is booked, but that a single segment of the award request is unavailable. You may want to try to book each segment separately, and once done, ask the airline to combine them for a single award. An example: A Delta award request from Dallas to Honolulu reads as not being available because the airline's booking engine would have only looked at Dallas-Los Angeles-Honolulu. So, try to book a flight segment from Dallas to Salt Lake City and then from Salt Lake City to Los Angeles and then book from Los Angeles to Honolulu. Once you have that done, request that the airline combine all the segment bookings into a single award. The good news is that this is still considered a single award redemption regardless of the number of segments it took to get the seat. In other words, this will cost you no more miles than if the award had been available on the Dallas-Los Angeles-Honolulu route.

1. Pick up the phone. Many programs have worked hard to convince members to book their awards online. The unfortunate problem with this is that most programs have faulty online award booking systems. Most do not include the award inventory for their airline partners. Most do not intelligently reroute a member through various hubs or city pairs. Most do not identify the problem with the award request such as a single segment not being available. Most do not allow you to register and be notified later on if a seat becomes available. Because of these limitations and more, we have no problem suggesting that if you have any problems booking an award online, you take the request to the phone line and try to work out the award through a reservation agent. Although most programs will now charge you to do this, we feel it is worth the cost.

BONUS TIP: Here is a bonus tip—a tactic of last resort that unfortunately should be in every frequent traveler's playbook.

If you have tried everything else and still cannot snag an award seat, consider bypassing capacity restrictions and parting with more miles to get an "any time" award. Generally priced at twice the number of miles required for a capacity controlled award, these unrestricted awards are much more plentiful than lower priced awards.

Redeeming 40,000 or 50,000 miles is a bitter pill to swallow if you have based your mileage earning campaign on the assumption that a free domestic ticket would be available for 25,000 miles or less. And if you simply do not have enough miles for an unrestricted award, the point is moot.

But, like it or not, more and more frequent flyers are being upsold to higher priced awards.

Now that we have ruined your day, we actually have some good news. Most program members only know how to "talk coach" when redeeming their miles—and for good reason as coach miles tend to go further. But if you are spending 40,000 to 50,000 miles for a coach award because none of the 25,000-mile awards are available, it is time to "talk first class." Here is why: In the Northwest WorldPerks program a saver award is 25,000 miles. A "Rule Buster" award for that same coach seat is 50,000 miles. Did you know that a saver first class ticket is only 45,000 miles? That is right. When coach is not available ask about the availability of a saver first class award before paying double miles for coach. In this example, you would have saved 5,000 miles and had a much better seat.

⊕ REMEMBER THIS:

▶ It is almost *Ripley's Believe It Or Not!*. On any given day, 100 percent of airline seats are available for award redemption.

▶ The past few years have been unusually tough on frequent flyers trying to cash in miles. This is mostly due to people redeeming awards solely to protect miles should an airline liquidate. Called ghost itineraries, people book an award ticket and then redeposit the miles back into their account once they know the airline is safe from liquidation. This takes up valuable award space from other members who actually want to use their miles for a free ticket.

▶ One of the best reasons for going that extra mile to earn elite status: Many programs waive blackout dates and capacity controls for their elite-level flyers.

Chapter 7

Keeping Tabs: Managing Your Loyalty Programs

THE TYPICAL FREQUENT TRAVELER PARTICIPATES in five or more airline and hotel programs. Within any one of those programs, opportunities to earn miles and points have multiplied beyond most individuals' abilities to keep pace. And the programs are constantly evolving, revising their policies, adding and losing partners, and sometimes even merging with other programs.

Still, as discussed at length in chapter 13 (Converting Miles and Points into Money), frequent flyer miles do have value, and anything with value is worth keeping track of. Therein lies the problem: How DOES the traveler keep track?

The type and extent of that tracking will—or should—depend on how actively a traveler pursues miles, as well as on how many programs in which he or she is enrolled.

What to Track

First, it is worth reviewing what should merit managing.

Consider the following:

Confirm That Miles Are Posted

While no industrywide figures are available, it is generally believed that more than 10 percent of all miles earned are never posted to a member's account. In some cases, the program's partners fail to capture the member's name or account number, or they fail to communicate the transaction to the program operator. In other cases, the program operator is the culprit, neglecting to credit the member's account with legitimately earned miles.

Such lapses are all but inevitable, even when travelers do their part to ensure their names and membership numbers are recorded for each mileage qualifying transaction. Because of this, consumers should make sure that all miles are posted. That means reconciling their accounts by retaining receipts or other records of mileage eligible transactions.

If miles or points fail to post, follow the program's instructions (which can be found on the program's Web site) for securing the missing credit.

Monitor Progress Toward Award Thresholds

Whether the goal is a quick coach flight to Toledo to visit Aunt Mary or a once-in-a-lifetime first class trip for two around the world with deluxe accommodations, be sure to keep track of your progress to get to the desired end.

To be prudent, continually reassess your travel goals. In light of the recent devaluation of frequent flyer miles and because of the financial instability roiling the airline industry, we recommend that travelers shift out of hoarding mode. In other words: Plan to use your miles sooner than later. Saving miles for travel during retirement—a common strategy—is a very risky proposition. (But for those of you who do save your miles, have comfort in knowing that one of *Mileage Pro*'s authors, Randy Petersen, is also saving his for retirement.)

Maintaining awareness of the number of miles remaining to be earned permits frequent flyers to prioritize their travels and mileage

Saving miles for travel during retirement is a very risky proposition.

redemption activities with an eye toward reaching their objective, whether that be free flights, elite perks or other coveted rewards.

Having achieved a targeted award, members should consider their next steps. What about another award or upgrade in the same program? Or perhaps it is time to start earning miles or hotel points in a different program that is a better fit for your earning or award priorities?

Monitor Progress Toward Earning Elite Status

If there is even a remote possibility of attaining elite status in an airline program (typically requiring 25,000 elite qualifying miles during a calendar year) then that is a goal a traveler should strive to achieve.

How many miles must I still earn in order to reach elite status? Which airlines can I fly in order to earn elite status in a particular program? In short, is it realistic to set elite status as a goal? And if it is, what is your plan for achieving it?

Frequent flyers should ask themselves: Now that I have reached entry-level elite status, should I now aim for the next tier? (As discussed in the chapter on elite status on page 98, there is an argument to be made for targeting elite status in a second program rather than striving for a higher elite tier in your primary program.)

Mileage Expiration Dates

Miles should never be allowed to expire. Period. That said consider this caveat: Because of the harsh expiration rules of Southwest, JetBlue and other discount carriers that terminate miles after just one or two years, we cannot say categorically that miles are only lost through inattention. Sometimes the loss is unavoidable.

With a generally liberal mileage expiration policy, miles get a new lease on life every time a single mile is earned or redeemed during a three-year period. Thus, miles in primary accounts—which are by definition active accounts—should not be at risk.

Miles most in danger of expiring are those in programs that are infrequently used. Those relatively inactive accounts should be regularly monitored for any impending expiration dates and action should be taken before the miles are terminated. For more information on expiring miles and points see chapter 15.

MEMORABLE MOMENTS
OF MILES & POINTS

NOVEMBER 1991
Pan Am ceases operation and the WorldPass frequent flyer program is merged with Delta's frequent flyer program.

Stay Abreast of Promotions

One key to making the most of loyalty program participation is to take advantage of the myriad of double, triple and other multi-mile bonus promotions consistently offered by the airlines, hotels and their partners.

There are opportunities to earn miles for many, if not most, everyday transactions. Additionally, many loyalty programs' partners will offer limited time bonuses such as double miles in American's program for renting from Avis or a free night certificate for new Marriott Rewards Visa card customers. Do not miss the bonus boat!

Program Changes

For better and for worse, loyalty programs are ever changing: In response to competitive pressures, in response to member feedback, and in response to economic cycles and business priorities.

It is worth reiterating that the fine print in the Terms & Conditions of every major loyalty program contains verbiage to the following effect: It is the member's responsibility to know and remain current with the program's rules, policies and operations.

That is not just a legal disclaimer. It is also good advice.

Staying Informed

Begin with the source: the airlines and hotels that sponsor the programs.

In fact, travelers can go a long way toward managing their program participation by simply reading the materials published by the programs themselves.

Driven by the impetus to both enhance service (by keeping members current) and to reduce costs (by reducing reliance on human customer service) airlines and hotels have digitized their programs, posting everything from Terms & Conditions to award catalogues on their Web sites. Additionally, account statements and promotional announcements are distributed via e-mail.

Sometimes, the airlines even offer bonus miles to encourage members to sign up to receive e-mail communications. Alaska

Airlines, for instance, recently offered Mileage Plan members 500 miles to subscribe to their member e-mail newsletter.

Some programs still send account statements via regular mail to members with recent activity, but more frequently, programs only provide statements by e-mail.

Whether online or on paper, a program's member communications is a must-read.

Mileage Management Software

For a number of mileage management activities, some software applications are specifically designed to make those chores both quicker and easier.

In the early days of the airline programs, the killer application for mileage trackers was a Lotus spreadsheet, with rows and columns depicting miles earned and redeemed in a traveler's preferred programs. But it was an imperfect solution because the information was only as current as the most recently mailed account statement (paper only in those days). The data had to be manually transferred from each statement onto the spreadsheet.

As can be said of so much else in travel, "the Internet changed all that." Today, in place of a homemade mileage spreadsheet, we have mileage tracking software that provides users with up-to-the-minute summaries of their miles, in one consolidated statement—immediately available with a single user name and password.

Users provide information on their frequent flyer accounts (member number and PIN) and grant limited power of attorney to the software's mileage manager to access their accounts. The software sends out digital agents over the Internet to "scrape" account information from airline and hotel Web sites. And the captured information—miles earned and redeemed, elite status levels and more—is then brought back and pasted into a master template.

Following are examples of several reputable mileage tracking software programs.

MileageManager (www.mileagemanager.com) consolidates statements from all major airline and hotel programs, plus those of American Express Membership Rewards and Diners Club Club Rewards. In addition to basic account information, this site lists program rules and bonus offers, and has an e-mail notification feature for program updates. Cost: $14.95 per year. [1]

MileageMiner (www.maxmiles.com) offers much the same functionality as MileageManager. Cost: $29.95 per year (after a free 90-day trial offer).

MileTracker (usatoday.deskport.biz) takes a different approach. Rather than storing the user's account information on a remote server, this data is kept on the user's own computer. Sponsored by *USA Today,* MileTracker is free.

Basic online account aggregators are also offered by several major banking and financial services companies. While these are designed principally to provide users with a comprehensive picture of their financial situation—assets from savings, checking

> **MEMORABLE MOMENTS OF MILES & POINTS**
>
> ## NOVEMBER 1991
>
> **As negotiations between Northwest Airlines and Midway Airlines fell apart,** Midway was unable to continue operations and discontinued its FlyersFirst program virtually overnight. The sudden collapse of the airline and its frequent flyer program left approximately 700,000 members holding millions of worthless miles, as no other program picked up the stranded members or their hard earned miles.

and brokerage accounts, and debits from credit cards, mortgages and other loans—they also allow for detailed tracking of travel rewards programs. In fact, to the extent that frequent flyer miles have value and are currency-like, the logic of monitoring reward accounts alongside banking and other dollar denominated accounts is compelling. Your Delta SkyMiles balance alongside your mortgage account details, alongside your Citibank MasterCard account, alongside your Starwood Preferred Guest points balance... all your assets (and liabilities) in one place! In some cases you must be a customer of the banking or financial services company, but no extra charge is imposed for using the online account managers offered by the likes of Fidelity Investments (called Full View), Citibank (called My Accounts Aggregation) and Bank of America (called My Portfolio)—all, incidentally, provided by Yodlee.

Independent Sources of Information and Advice

Last, but hardly least, mileage earners are privy to a number of independent publications devoted specifically to helping consumers stay abreast of frequent traveler program developments. Some are written and published by the authors and publisher of this book (as noted below).

Web sites

- WebFlyer.com is a self-described "information portal for frequent flyer news, promotions, services, interactive features and much more." [1]

- InsideFlyer.com is the online version of *InsideFlyer* magazine. [1]

- FlyerTalk.com is without question the largest,

busiest online travel forum on the Internet. Although this site started with a strict focus on discussions of mileage related topics, it has expanded to cover other aspects of travel as well, including cruises, traveling with children and airport security. [1]

- FrequentFlier.com features coverage of the latest promotions and program changes as well as commentary and advice on managing miles and points. Also popular on the site is a discussion area dubbed the FrequentFlier Forum. [2]

- While SmarterTravel.com is not exclusively focused on miles and points, the site covers the topic with regularly updated news and advice. Its nifty database-driven search tool displays promotional offers categorized by program and partner.

- FrequentFlyer.oag.com lists monthly program reward promotions and offers periodic Mileage Q&As on subjects such as airline bankruptcy, credit card miles, and miles and points redemption strategies. The site also has a free biweekly e-newsletter (*OAG Frequent Flyer Update*) that provides loyalty program deals and Mileage Q&As. [3]

Links to these and other Web sites can be found in the Resources for Mileage Junkies chapter on page 183.

E-mail Newsletters

Three e-mail newsletters provide news, information and advice specifically for participants in frequent travel programs. They are:

- The FrequentFlier Crier (weekly) [2]
- MilesLink (weekly) [1]

    ✦ MileAlert (published biweekly by SmarterTravel.com).

All three free newsletters cover loyalty program changes, promotions and best practices.

Again, links to these and other general travel-oriented newsletters appear in the Resources for Mileage Junkies chapter.

The Magazine

InsideFlyer is the only printed publication of its type: a monthly magazine devoted exclusively to coverage of travel awards programs. A subscription is $45 per year. [1]

The Frequent Flyer Guide

Another print publication, *The Official Frequent Flyer Guidebook*, contains more than 400 pages of detailed terms and conditions on 30-plus major loyalty programs. Cost: $14.95. [1]

⊕ REMEMBER THIS:

- Never assume that miles will be properly posted to your account. Often they are not. Retain receipts and boarding passes until you have confirmed that miles were credited to your account.

- Stay abreast of program changes and limited time promotions. Read the newsletters and other materials sent out by your programs as well as those from independent publishers.

- And do not forget to register to receive bonuses; now a requirement of most promotional offers.

[1] Part of the WebFlyer network owned by Randy Petersen, co-author of this book.
[2] Written and published by Tim Winship, co-author of this book.
[3] Published by *Frequent Flyer* magazine, which is owned by the publisher of this book, OAG Worldwide Inc.

Chapter 8

Exchanging Miles and Points Among Programs

SOMETIME DURING YOUR MILEAGE CAREER you will likely need to exchange miles or points between programs. Generally this is due to one of several circumstances:

- You are short the number of miles necessary for an award and need to add miles to your (or a traveling companion's) account to qualify for the redemption. This is known as "topping off."

- You may be worried about the longevity of your miles or points based on the possible bankruptcy or liquidation of your preferred program. As a result, you want to try to guard your miles and points by transferring them to a "safe" program that is less at risk to go bankrupt or to liquidate.

- You started earning miles a long time ago and, thanks to the information in this book, you now know that you are better off concentrating your miles or points into a single account, or, at most, into a small number of preferred accounts. You can clean up your accounts by transferring small amounts of miles or points (often called "orphans") into a single account or into those few preferred programs.

- You are in danger of miles expiring in one of your "infrequent" programs. Exchanging miles or points into that account will qualify as an "activity" and will keep those miles from expiring.

- You are having problems getting an award ticket with one airline so you would like to take advantage of another airline's promotional offer. You want to transfer your miles, and even some of your hotel points, into another airline program for a one-time redemption.

- Your preferred and secondary programs are now partners in an alliance and you are wondering how to move miles/points from one to the other.

- Your primary programs have changed because of a job transfer. Unfortunately, the airline in which you have earned all your miles does not fly from your new city of residence.

Exchanging miles or points between programs is possible though it is not a particularly pleasant or rewarding experience. While the principle is the same, it is nowhere near as easy as exchanging your dollars for pounds or Euros.

MEMORABLE MOMENTS OF MILES 8 POINTS

OCTOBER 1994

Hilton HHonors introduces the HHonors Reward Exchange. The benefit is unique in that members can convert airline miles into HHonors points AND they can convert HHonors points into airline miles. The partners in the program at inception included Alaska Airlines, America West Airlines, Delta Air Lines, United Airlines, American Express Membership Miles and Diners Club Club Rewards.

The reason? The premise of these programs is to promote loyalty. By encountering barriers to exchanging miles or points, members are convinced that the best way to earn benefits and free awards is to remain loyal to one program. If American AAdvantage and Southwest Rapid Rewards miles and credits were freely exchangeable, those living in Dallas or any other market would have no reason to choose one airline over the other. In that context, open exchanges simply do not make sense.

How to Exchange Miles and Points between Accounts

To exchange miles and points, you will need the assistance of a "middleman": a program or conduit that will allow you to switch from one program's currency to another. Be prepared for "sticker shock" though. Your miles are almost guaranteed to lose value, and thus the reason we discourage exchanges.

In most cases, because of the ease in earning miles, we think it is best for you to consider going up in value not down. For instance, in a press release by Points.com, their average exchange in the second quarter of 2005 was 17,380 miles/points. That is a lot of miles to be exchanging. In fact, exchanging that amount within Points.com would likely leave you with less than 2,000 miles in another program. As a further example, exchanging that amount through the Hilton HHonors Reward Exchange would give you between 3,000 and 5,000 miles. Using Club Rewards by Diners Club, you would still lose half of the miles with which you started.

In a day when some members decry that frequent flyer programs have become "devalued," self selecting to devalue your miles even more through the use of a middleman might be considered a poor decision.

The Middleman Process				
5,000 American AAdvantage miles	=	10,000 Hilton HHonors points	=	1,000 Continental OnePass miles

Before we get into the middleman process, keep in mind that a growing trend in airline and hotel programs is to allow members to exchange miles and points between one person's account to another person's. In the past, this was seen as a huge "no no." Now, programs such as American AAdvantage and InterContinental Priority Club Rewards will allow members, for a fee, to exchange miles and points between accounts with no loss of value to the miles and points. This might be a new option for you, but remember, it is only for sharing miles or points within a particular program.

Essentially there are four types of exchanges: miles to miles, miles to points, points to miles and points to points.

The easiest is to transfer points into miles. All major hotel loyalty programs offer conversions from points to miles. Still, do not be fooled. The drawback is that each hotel has its own way to value the exchange based on the program's earning ratio.

For instance, Priority Club Rewards exchanges points into miles at a ratio of four points to one mile. The Starwood Preferred Guest program converts their points into airline miles at a one-to-one ratio. Is Starwood four times richer in a mileage exchange? No. The Starwood program earns points at a rate of two points per dollar spent, while Priority Club Rewards earns 10 points per dollar spent. Therefore, carefully examine the value of the points you have before exchanging. Knowing the earning rate of each program prior to any exchange should be your first step. This example may change if the miles you are seeking had been earned as an elite member, or if you are exchanging more than 20,000 points (see below). Still, the lesson remains constant: Do your homework before exchanging a single mile or point.

Perhaps an easier way to understand this is if you were to spend $1,000 in each of these two hotel programs. $1,000 spent at Priority Club hotels would earn you 10,000 points based on an earning rate of 10 points per dollar spent. At Starwood hotels that same $1,000 would earn you only 2,000 points (two points for every dollar spent). If you were to then convert the points in each program to miles, you would earn 2,500 miles from converting Priority Club points while earning only 2,000 miles when converting Starwood points. With Priority Club, four points convert to one mile, while with Starwood, one point converts to one mile.

Now, using the same example, change the scenario to spending $10,000 as elite members in each program. In the case of Starwood, elite members earn three points per dollar spent so the total number of points earned is 30,000. For Priority Club, Gold Elite members earn an additional 10 percent bonus on points earned, so spending $10,000 will earn you

110,000 points. (Remember: You earn 10 Priority Club points per dollar spent.) Converting 110,000 points with Priority Club earns you 27,500 miles. Converting Starwood points into miles earns you 35,000 miles. In Starwood's program, all members who convert 20,000 Starwood points into miles receive an additional 5,000 miles. As you can see, the advantage is now with Starwood but it gets even more complicated because if the Priority Club elite member was Platinum instead of Gold, he or she would earn a 50 percent bonus, thus earning a total of 150,000 points from the $10,000 spent. Those points converted into miles would be 37,500. Now, aren't you glad you bought this book?

The next two situations are similar in that they each require the use of a "middleman." There are five exchange options in North America: Amtrak Guest Awards, Diners Club Club

Bonus tip: With Starwood, never redeem 45,000 points at one time because you only get the 5,000-mile bonus converting 20,000. For example, if you have 45,000 Starwood points, convert 20,000 and then another 20,000 in a separate transaction. By doing this you walk away with 10,000 more miles.

Rewards, Hilton HHonors Reward Exchange, Priority Club Rewards and Points.com. Note: Other than Points.com, these programs were not designed to be exchange programs. They are travel rewards programs that, when used in a particular way, allow members to convert or exchange points into miles, miles into points, or miles into points and then into miles in another airline program.

Amtrak Guest Awards: The first priority of this program is to build Amtrak passenger loyalty, but because of the richness of the program, there are opportunities to use it as a conduit to exchange miles between different airlines and hotel points between various hotels. The big caveat: This only works for a limited number of programs including Continental OnePass, Hilton HHonors and Midwest Airlines Midwest Miles. The benefit of exchanging airline miles through Amtrak is that Continental and Midwest Airlines do not provide a way for you to convert miles between their programs, therefore, you are using Amtrak as the "middleman." Also, Hilton HHonors points convert at a ratio of 10,000 HHonors points to 1,500 Amtrak Guest Rewards points, whereas miles convert at a one-to-one ratio with Amtrak Guest Rewards points.

If making use of every earned mile is important to you, we will illustrate a way to save 5,000 miles. In the Continental OnePass program, a free ticket to Mexico is available to members for 35,000 miles. However, you could get to Mexico for free if you only had 30,000 miles. Using the Amtrak Guest Rewards program as your middleman, you would convert your 30,000 miles from OnePass into Guest Rewards points on a one-to-one basis and then convert those points on a one-to-one basis to Midwest Airlines' Midwest Miles program. (You must be a member of both programs for this to work.) You will now have 30,000 Midwest Miles miles and a free ticket to Mexico using Midwest Airlines' partner Frontier Airlines, which only requires 30,000 miles to go to Mexico. You saved 5,000 miles, which would have been required if you had wanted to redeem your OnePass miles and go to Mexico on Continental. Sure, it takes a little work, but 5,000 miles saved is, well, 5,000 miles saved. Now, it is a little tricky because Amtrak limits exchanges to only 25,000 miles per calendar year (unless you are an Amtrak Guest Rewards Select member in which case you are allowed to exchange more than 25,000 miles annually). If you were interested in the above example, you would need to plan the exchange at the end of the year, exchanging 25,000 miles in December and another 5,000 miles in January, and, of course, January is about the right time to redeem an award to Mexico. One hint: Do yourself a favor and make sure the award seats on the flights you want are available before you do all of this work.

That said, in some instances there is more to exchanges than just miles to miles. Members may consider exchanging miles from OnePass and Midwest Miles to Amtrak to garner other award choices such as hotel room awards with Hilton, Marriott, Sheraton, Westin and Ritz-Carlton, as well as gift certificates to places like The Home Depot and Ruth's Chris Steak House—awards not offered by either of Amtrak's airline partners Continental and Midwest Airlines.

The process is similar to any other middleman exchange. A member exchanges his or her OnePass miles into Amtrak Guest Rewards points. He or she can then choose to further exchange those points for airline miles with Midwest Airlines and redeem a free flight. Or, he or she can choose to convert these new Amtrak Guest Rewards points for points within the Hilton HHonors program and redeem a free night. The process is always the same. The choice of what you have decided to exchange to is the differentiator.

There are other choices you do not even want to consider. For instance, 25,000 OnePass miles will earn you one week's car rental from Hertz. We do not believe this is of great value since that same 25,000 miles could be redeemed for a free airline ticket, which would typically cost more than the car rental.

Also, 22,500 Midwest Miles could get you one free night at a level three Starwood Hotel—a nice hotel, but not worth a free airline ticket.

Diners Club Club Rewards: This exchange middleman is one we rarely suggest because it only will work if you are a Diners Club cardholder. This means you must invest $95 to acquire the card, diluting the value of the exchange for most people.

If you are an existing cardholder, you can enact exchanges from both American AAdvantage and United Mileage Plus. You will receive 5,000 Club Rewards points for every 10,000 miles you convert. Conversions must be made in 10,000-mile increments with a conversion limit of 50,000 miles in one calendar year, per partner. Since Club Rewards exchanges their points to miles on a one-to-one basis, this means you can convert AAdvantage and Mileage Plus to miles in other programs with only a 50 percent devaluation. (That devaluation is because 10,000 miles equals only 5,000 Club Reward points.) Remember, though, that there are fees involved, both with the card's annual charge and with the government induced fee of 95 cents for every 2,000 points.

Hilton HHonors Reward Exchange: This is the original exchange option. While many airlines have pulled out, this option can still be useful in certain situations. Currently among the U.S. programs that exchange miles for hotel points only American AAdvantage, Midwest Airlines Midwest Miles and Hawaiian Airlines HawaiianMiles participate. Others include Virgin Atlantic, Mexicana and LAN. The exchange ratio is 5,000 miles into 10,000 HHonors points, but 10,000 HHonors points will only gain you 1,500 miles when you convert back into miles—a devaluation of 70 percent. We think the best way to use this program is to exchange miles for hotel rooms rather than go from miles to hotel points and then back to miles in another airline program, or even just going from points to miles. Note: You must be a member of Hilton HHonors to use the Hilton HHonors Reward Exchange program. Also note: If you want to exchange HHonors points for miles the selection of airlines is greater and includes the airlines listed above, as well as British Airways, Continental and Delta among others.

Priority Club Rewards: Not many know you can use this program as a conduit. The choices are extremely limited, but they exist. Priority Club Rewards members can redeem American AAdvantage miles into Priority Club Rewards at a ratio of 1,000 miles to 800 points. You can then convert these points into miles with a variety of domestic and international airline programs, usually at a ratio of four points to one mile. Thus 10,000 AAdvantage miles would become 2,000 miles in another airline program—a devaluation of some 80 percent.

Points.com: Your last option for transferring miles is Points.com. While this program started out as an exchange, a recent change in strategy is trying to convert it into a "rewards management portal." This means it is a little more difficult to determine the conversion rates and strategies for converting your miles and hotel points. Also, some airlines, such as Delta SkyMiles and US Airways Dividend Miles, do not allow travelers to "swap out" their miles though members can "swap in." ("Swapping in" is a term that Points.com uses. Loyalty program members can use Points.com to swap their Midwest Airlines miles into Delta SkyMiles miles but they cannot swap back out their Delta SkyMiles for Midwest Airlines miles.) Because frequent flyer programs themselves set their own conversion ratios rather than Points.com doing so, no concrete formula is available. You will have to enroll on Points.com to test the most current exchange rates. Past exchanges show devaluations of up to 92 percent. Points.com membership fees are associated with exchanges including, but not limited to, processing fees.

As noted at the beginning of this chapter, many factors are to be considered when planning an exchange of miles and hotel points. We present options for you, but feel very strongly that you can learn to manage even a small amount of miles to your benefit without exchanging through a middleman and losing miles.

Here is an example: In the fall of 2005, members of the Northwest WorldPerks program could redeem their miles along with some cash for airline tickets. Commonly known as "Cash & Miles," this promotion allows members with a minimal amount of miles to enjoy rewards. For instance, in the Northwest WorldPerks offer, members with 5,000 miles could travel to Florida from certain destinations in the United States using 5,000 miles plus $149. That is an excellent way to save money since 5,000 miles through an exchange program (also referred to as a middleman) would likely only equal 500 miles in another airline program. WorldPerks members with 10,000 miles could have flown to Florida for only $99 or to other destinations in the United States for $109 to $199. Generally speaking, you would not have been able to purchase any ticket for less money. Sometimes it is far better to purchase the number of miles you need to get to an award level rather than dilute the miles you have by going through an exchange.

Other types of exchanges are fairly common, but can be risky. Many members exchange miles and hotels points among themselves. It is not uncommon for a member of one program to "exchange" an award with a friend having miles or points in another program. While this certainly straddles the fine line between "bartering," which is against some programs' rules, it does present an alternative. For instance, maybe a traveler has miles with the Delta SkyMiles program and wants to go to Australia. Delta and its partners do not provide a convenient way to get there without routing through northern Asia. The member might consider borrowing miles from a friend who has miles in another airline program that offers direct flights to Australia. (Any member of a major U.S. loyalty program can transfer an award into another person's name.) The traveler would then owe his or her friend the same number of miles for a Delta award later on. Also, someone with a lot of airline miles may exchange flight awards to a friend in exchange for hotel awards. But again, in some programs this amounts to bartering and may be prohibited. Check your program's rules. Note: Transferring an award to someone without "strings attached" (such as in the case of a gift) is fully permissible. When we say that an exchange might amount to bartering, we are referring to a "strings attached" type of exchange.

Finally, there are exchanges of miles for money. You may have heard of "coupon brokers" who promise get-rich-quick schemes by trading your unused miles and points into cash. But, this type of transaction is prohibited in the rules of every frequent flyer program in the world.

These coupon brokers advertise heavily on the Internet and in newspaper ads by claiming there is no "law" against such a transaction. Law or no law, this type of transaction is very much against the rules of every loyalty program. Almost daily, members are busted for buying and selling miles for cash. As a result, airlines can close accounts, leaving members with no recourse. For more discussion on buying and selling frequent flyer awards through coupon brokers see chapter 14.

⊕ REMEMBER THIS:

- When possible, exchanging miles and points between various programs may not always be a pleasant or rewarding experience. Truth be told: It is much easier to exchange your dollars for pounds or Euros.

- There are four types of exchanges: miles to miles (hardest), miles to points, points to miles (easiest), and points to points.

- Many members exchange miles and points among themselves. It is not uncommon for a member of one program to "exchange" an award with a friend having miles or points in another program.

Chapter 9

Elite Status

IF FREE TRAVEL IS THE heart of frequent flyer programs, elite status is the soul of these programs. After all, loyalty programs are about increasing revenues and profits, but not all customers contribute equally to a company's bottom line.

This fact is embodied in a key principle of loyalty marketing, Pareto's Principle, named for the 18th century Italian economist, Vilfredo Pareto, who observed that 80 percent of a country's wealth was controlled by 20 percent of its population. In business, that idea, often known as the 80-20 rule, suggests that a select few consumers are responsible for a disproportionately large share of a company's profits.

In the travel industry that group is comprised of business travelers. They travel often, and they generally purchase the highest priced airline tickets, bought at the last minute, and free of the restrictions that leisure travelers endure in order to get the lowest possible prices.

So, while the programs are designed to provide a payoff for occasional customers, the real target of loyalty marketing is business travelers.

That is where elite status comes in. It is a special package of recognition and benefits reserved for a program's most profitable members—a sort of "super program" within a program.

The goal behind awarding those shiny silver, gold and platinum colored cards—and the special rewards and recognition that come with them—is to maximize the number of business travelers patronizing a particular airline or hotel chain, and to maximize the spending of each and every one of those high yield customers.

Obviously, there is no rule that limits elite status to only those traveling exclusively on business. Anyone who meets the entry requirements—for most airlines that is 25,000 elite qualifying miles (EQMs) flown during a year—can reap the rewards. And those rewards make gaining elite status a worthwhile priority.

The Benefits of Elite

Of course, there is an element of pride associated with being recognized among an airline's most frequent flyers. But there are more tangible rewards; upgrades first among them.

Upgrades

By definition, elite program members are constant frequent flyers. Most are business travelers, logging significant time on the road on assignments for companies that pay their salaries. Nothing can so effectively mitigate the discomfort and aggravation of relentless travel as a big, wide seat in the front of the plane.

MEMORABLE MOMENTS OF MILES & POINTS

AUGUST 1990

Alaska Airlines introduces its Most Valuable Passenger (MVP) elite level. No qualification criteria were established as MVP status was strictly invitation-only. Among the benefits conferred on MVP members: a 50 percent mileage bonus, a special customer service line, and the ability to redeem 5,000 miles for a first class upgrade from any published fare.

Thus, airlines have featured upgrades as the central benefit for attaining elite status.

There are three important variables when considering elite upgrades: Whether the upgrades are complimentary or earned; whether the upgrades are from most published fares or only from prohibitively expensive full coach fares; and how far in advance the upgrades can be confirmed.

Standard policy among larger full service airlines is to offer elite members, on a space available basis, unlimited complimentary upgrades from coach to business or first class on flights within North America.

Among the major carriers, Continental, Delta, Northwest and US Airways offer their elite members complimentary upgrades from most discounted coach fares. Members of American and United's programs can only use their complimentary upgrades when flying on full-fare coach tickets.

When booking upgrades, the general rule is that higher level elites can confirm upgrades sooner than lower level elites. This gives them better odds of securing an upgraded seat. So, while a top elite member might be able to lock in an upgrade five days, or even a week, in advance of a flight's departure date, lower tier elites must wait until 24 hours before the flight to establish an upgrade.

Elite Bonus Miles

Elite members earn bonus miles for flights on the airline in which they established elite status and selected partner airlines (typically airlines participating in the same global alliance). Read chapter 11 for more information on the global alliances.

The bonus amount depends on the elite level, with higher levels receiving a larger bonus. Most often, the top two elite levels earn a 100 percent bonus while the lowest level members earn a 25 percent bonus.

The elite bonus is computed as a percentage of the base miles, which are the miles actually flown, or, for shorter flights, the minimum miles (usually 500) awarded per flight. The elite bonus calculation does not include class-of-service bonuses (awarded for first and business class flights) or promotional bonuses. While the bonus is referred to as an "elite bonus," the extra miles do not count toward elite status.

Award Travel Blackouts Waived

When it comes time to redeem your miles for a free trip, many programs eliminate blackout dates and/or increase award seat availability for elite members.

Preferred Check-In

Elite members are normally entitled to check in at the airlines' first or business class counters even when traveling on a coach ticket.

Priority Boarding and Preferred Seating

Priority boarding allows elite members to be among the first onboard, a bonus since that is when there is still space available in the overhead bins for carry-on bags. This proves to be a very welcome perk when traveling in coach on a full flight. Some airlines also set aside better seats on the aircraft for elite members such as with United's roomier Economy Plus rows specifically reserved for elites and full-fare ticket holders.

Priority Security Lanes

One of the most recent perks given to elite members: access to special lines to quickly clear airport security checkpoints.

Airport Lounge Benefits

Elite members enjoy discounted rates on annual airport lounge memberships. Delta, for instance, sells Crown Room Club memberships—normally $475 per year—to Silver Medallion members for $350 and to Gold members for $275. Platinum members pay nothing.

Dedicated Customer Service

Most programs make available to their elite members—or at least to their highest level elites—a direct customer service phone line that handles VIP calls exclusively. Elites can expect to get through to an agent faster and receive a higher level of service than the norm. When your flight is cancelled and you need to rebook an alternative flight, this preferential treatment can be a lifesaver.

Credit Card Benefits

A significant benefit to those who make frequent use of their airline credit cards is the maximum number of miles earned for credit card purchases being raised or eliminated altogether. Example: Non-elites are limited to earning a maximum of 60,000 miles per year for charges on the United Mileage Plus Signature

Visa. Mileage Plus Premier, Premier Executive and Premier Executive 1K members are exempt from these mileage limits.

How Many Miles?

Through the years, airlines have made periodic attempts to measure loyalty in dollar terms through the cost of tickets. However, the tracking was problematic and the idea never gained traction.

The current standard measures of loyalty are elite qualifying miles, sometimes in combination with booked cabin classes (such as business or first), and secondly, flight segments (one-way flights).

A typical airline program with three elite levels would award elite status based on the following criteria:

Elite Tier	Qualification Criteria	
	Elite Qualifying Miles	Flight Segments
Low	25,000	30
Medium	50,000	60
High	75,000-100,000	100

The above qualification scheme is, of course, a generalization. Specifics differ among the programs.

American Airlines, for example, has a points system in addition to elite qualifying miles and segments. This gives greater weight to more expensive fare types, allowing travelers who routinely buy expensive unrestricted tickets to reach elite status faster.

Continental, Delta, Northwest and United award a 50 percent elite qualifying mileage bonus and double points for more expensive tickets (unrestricted coach, business and first class fares).

In most programs, elite qualifying miles are those miles

actually flown on the host airline (the airline operating the frequent flyer program in question) and on the host airline's partner airlines.

In the programs of the largest airlines, members can also earn elite qualifying miles on partner carriers that participate in a given airline's global alliance. These global alliance partners are considered "preferred" carriers.

American's preferred partners are the oneworld airlines; Delta's are the SkyTeam carriers (including Continental and Northwest); and United's are the Star Alliance airlines. Smaller carriers, which do not participate in global alliances, tend to designate as preferred partners those airlines with which they have codeshare agreements or other joint marketing programs.

The Qualification and Membership Periods

Elite status is awarded for miles earned during a calendar year, and in most cases remains in effect from the date it is earned until the end of February of the second year following the qualification year.

Status earned for travel between January 1 and December 31, 2005, would remain in effect until February 28, 2007.

Other Sources of Elite Qualifying Miles

While flight miles on the host airline (the airline in which you have elite status) remain the principal source for elite miles, it is worth mentioning that miles from other sources are increasingly being counted toward elite status. This development reflects the recognition by airlines that loyalty program members can make significant contributions to airlines' bottom lines even through non-flight activities. Miles earned through non-flight activities generate substantial revenues for the airlines that host the programs. Current and would-be elites should be on the lookout for opportunities to earn elite qualifying miles through credit card use, by booking on the airlines' Web sites, and via other non-traditional sources.

Elite Matching and Challenges

There is another tactic for attaining elite status that is little known outside the ranks of very frequent flyers: Just ask for it.

For years, airlines have engaged in elite matching—on a request basis by offering elite members of competitive programs comparable status in their program. The process is straightforward. The traveler seeking elite status contacts the customer service center of the targeted airline's program and asks if they will match elite status earned with a different airline. If so, the member will be asked to fax a recent statement showing that he or she is indeed qualified as elite in the other carrier's program. Assuming the documentation supports the request, status is granted.

Not all airlines match other carriers' elite status. Those that do match do so selectively, focusing on their primary competitors. Airlines that partner together in a global alliance typically will not "elite match" each other. The unwritten rule: Do not poach your partner's customers.

Elite matching should not be taken lightly. Carriers generally will not honor a second matching request from the same member.

Million Milers

In addition to earning elevated status for a limited time by reaching certain thresholds during a 12-month period, American, Delta and United recognize customers who have earned a million miles or more over the course of their memberships.

In American's program, members receive lifetime Gold elite status after accruing one million miles and Platinum after two million no matter how those miles are earned.

By contrast, in Delta's program, only elite qualifying miles count toward earning Million Miler status, which awards permanent Silver, Gold and Platinum Medallion status after reaching one, two and four million miles, respectively.

United bestows lifetime Premier Executive status on Mileage Plus members who fly one million miles on United, United Express or Ted. Note: You can earn United elite qualifying miles on United Express and Ted.

Hotel Programs' Elite

We have focused on elite status in airline programs because that topic tends to be the primary focus of hard-core frequent travelers. But, while it might not be their first priority, most credentialed frequent flyers also make it a point to maintain elite status in one or more hotel programs.

Hotels' best customers are the very same frequent travelers targeted by the airlines' elite programs. And since hotel programs were modeled after the airline programs, it should come as no surprise that hotel programs also have elite tiers and that their featured elite benefits are room upgrades and bonus points.

Hotel programs award entry-level elite status for as few as 10 nights stayed during the qualification period, which is generally a calendar year. Top level status is earned after 50 to 75 nights.

In programs with two tiers, complimentary room upgrades are offered to all elites (Starwood Preferred Guest, Gold Crown Club International), or just to members of the top tier (Hyatt Gold Passport, Priority Club Rewards).

In programs with three tiers (Hilton HHonors, Marriott Rewards), upgrades are offered to members in the top two elite tiers.

Depending on the program and the tier, elite members earn points bonuses of between 10 and 50 percent.

Other elite benefits vary among programs and may include late checkout, guaranteed room availability, a dedicated customer service phone line and check cashing privileges.

Is There Gold in Your Future?

Elite status is not for everyone so be realistic about your need to reach elite and your ability to reach this goal. Earning 25,000 elite qualifying miles in a year is by no means impossible, especially with the current trend toward awarding EQMs for non-flight activity. But if elite status is not a viable option, do not sweat it. There is no pressing need to carry a Gold card if your annual travel is limited to a couple of short-haul flights to visit friends and family.

On the other hand, if elite status seems just out of reach, it may simply be a matter of fine tuning your efforts to get there.

This is the appropriate place to reiterate the following advice: Make it a priority to consolidate your mileage earning into a single program. Earnings spread among multiple programs can undermine a member's efforts to reach elite status as well as his or her pursuit of awards. In fact, because there is a 12-month window to reach elite, the pressure is even greater to consolidate.

It is a good idea to begin each year by reviewing a list of program partners that award elite qualifying miles. Then, whenever possible, confine your travel to those partners. For example, if you are aiming for elite status in United's Mileage

Plus program and you have a trip planned to Amsterdam, fly on United and Lufthansa via Frankfurt rather than nonstop on KLM. The United/Lufthansa combination will earn elite qualifying miles in Mileage Plus whereas the KLM flight will not.

Take stock of your situation as the year winds down. If you are within striking distance of reaching elite, perhaps that trip planned for early next year can be rescheduled for this year. Or consider making a "mileage run"—a trip taken for the sole purpose of earning miles. Since the goal is to earn the miles for the lowest possible per mile price, likely candidates would be off-season, advance purchase roundtrips to Europe or Asia—an extremely cost effective way to reach elite status or to upgrade from a lower to a higher elite tier. Note: Most low cost tickets to Europe or Asia earn elite qualifying miles.

If you fly enough to qualify for elite status in an airline program, it is likely that you will also stand a good chance of reaching elite status in a hotel program. Just as we have advocated participating in a hotel program as a logical complement to an airline program, so we also recommend augmenting airline elite perks with the elite benefits associated with hotel programs.

⊕ REMEMBER THIS:

- ⟩ The principal benefit of elite status is upgrades.

- ⟩ In most programs, entry-level elite status is reached after earning 25,000 elite qualifying miles (EQMs) during a calendar year.

- ⟩ If you fly enough to come within striking distance of earning elite status, make it a priority to qualify. If not, do not sweat it. You probably do not fly enough to need upgrades.

- ⟩ There are two ways to attain elite status: the old-fashioned way by earning elite qualifying miles or segments, and through the back door by petitioning to have your status upgraded.

Chapter 10

Moving Up: The Matter of Upgrades

REPEAT AFTER US: HE WHO hesitates sits in coach. He who fails to rack up miles sits in coach. He who fails to follow the rules sits in coach.

Now repeat after us: He who pays attention and follows the "code" will (usually) get to sit up front.

Actually, it might be said that some frequent flyers develop the dreaded "FOC" (fear of coach) syndrome after years of travel in the sky. Basically, it is a play on the idea that a REAL frequent flyer never sits in coach because he or she always has the miles and the knowledge of the system to sit up front.

But let's face it: Domestic first class, if there even is one, is slowly becoming worthless whereas internationally the frequent traveler will find it is worth every effort to get an upgrade. It is not just about free drinks and slightly bigger seats; it is more about finer wines, a choice of something more than beef or chicken and seats that convert into beds. If you strive for an upgrade, do it on an international flight.

There are generally four types of upgrades: the complimentary ones you receive as a member of an airline's highest elite level; those you "purchase" in exchange for miles; those you buy from an airline for about $25 to $75 for 500- to 1,000-mile segments (segments being actual miles flown); and those you grovel for.

Note: Upgrade awards using miles are not based on distance, so it would probably be a poor use of miles to upgrade to first class on a short flight from Chicago to Milwaukee. It would be a good use of miles to upgrade from Boston to San Diego. Both examples require the same number of miles if you are a Northwest WorldPerks member—5,000 miles each way when upgrading from full-fare coach to first class, or 15,000 miles each way when upgrading from select coach fares.

A number of frequent flyers believe the only way they can upgrade is by using miles. Other options are available but you should consider the real cost before purchasing. For example, it often takes at least $250 to earn 1,000 miles from flying. It costs $1,000 to earn 1,000 miles with an airline credit card. That is why we suggest purchasing segment upgrades (often $100 will get you 1,000 miles of upgrade) rather than cashing in your miles. Segment upgrades are upgrades based on distances flown, unlike mileage upgrades that are simply an award from any city to another within a particular zone; for instance, North America to Hawaii.

Many major airlines will offer a complimentary upgrade to members when they fly on a full-fare coach ticket. This is a hot topic because it is an area where airlines can leverage against most low cost carriers, but at the expense of elite members who no longer can upgrade as often as in years past. This is because by giving away upgrades based on fare cost, there is more demand for the upgrades, thus taking away first class seats from the highest level elite members who have earned the privilege of free upgrades.

Is a free upgrade still possible? Rarely. Because of the way the airline industry has changed the type of aircraft they fly, you are more likely to find yourself on an RJ (regional jet) without any first class cabin.

Finally, what about that groveling? Most airlines state, in no uncertain terms, that their policies prohibit arbitrary upgrading, both at check-in and onboard. This is a firm rule, with no room for negotiation or interpretation. This becomes understandable when you consider that upgrading is now often done electronically, rather than by queuing up at the check-in counter.

MEMORABLE MOMENTS OF MILES & POINTS

AUGUST 1986

The Phoenix Suns, the Portland Trailblazers and the Seattle Supersonics tell players that in the future the NBA club will claim all frequent flyer miles when the teams travel. The players' union threatens to make mileage awards a bargaining issue. Suns players refuse to autograph team photographs or make promotional appearances until the policy is scrapped.

While it seems this is the general policy of most airlines, there is a mysteriously privileged group who repeatedly (and smugly) report after traveling they were "bumped up." We suspect some of this is bradaggio but nonetheless, here are reasons to keep the faith.

If the flight is relatively empty your chances are slim. Even though seats in business class may also be empty, the airlines usually do not upgrade people for no reason because doing so will set a precedent the frequent flyer will expect every time. As well, gate attendants and flight attendants are employed for other reasons than trying to decide who gets the next upgrade.

If the flight is full, your chances are better. Airlines carefully plan how much they oversell flights, and their inventory departments are not upset if people need to be upgraded to accommodate everybody on the flight. Therefore, on a full flight the airlines sometimes are forced to upgrade people. In this scenario, if you have a good story, you may be lucky. Remember of course that business or first class may already be full from pre-booked, elite-level upgrades.

Volunteer to give up your seat if the flight is oversold in coach. Tell the agent that if the airline needs your seat for people flying on standby you will gladly give up your seat and upgrade to first class. These are called operational upgrades, and while it would seem logical that the most senior elite member who is still sitting in coach would be upgraded, there is very little time for the gate agent to check the manifest. Your gesture may make it easier for the airline to make an on-time departure. Also, the airline is less likely to upgrade someone flying standby than you as those on standby most likely purchased very cheap tickets. Small chance, but worth a try. If the airline ends up needing your seat for someone else, ask if you can be upgraded on the next flight.

If you have been inconvenienced by the airline do not hesitate to ask for an upgrade. Again, airlines do not generally upgrade people for no reason, but if they have caused you a problem, that may be reason enough.

Do not wait until you are onboard. The flight attendants usually do not have the authority to upgrade people because they do not know the details of your ticket.

It is highly unlikely that you will be upgraded if you are traveling on a free frequent flyer reward ticket in coach. The airlines do not like it when people try to redeem only enough points for a coach ticket and then try to sweet talk their way to an upgrade. If you try this approach, you will often be the last person considered for an upgrade.

Some other considerations:

Timing
One major secret to getting an upgrade is in knowing when you can secure an upgrade. For most members, it is either 24, 48 or 72 hours in advance for a confirmed upgrade.

Simple enough? Not quite.

Airlines differ in when they begin the actual countdown. For some, you count backward from the day of departure, which starts at 12:00 a.m. (often EST). For others, you start counting the hours from the time of your flight's scheduled departure. Work the time differential to your advantage.

If you really want to get a jump on the competition, time your call to capitalize on any time zone differentials. Find out the service center's location and place your call to coincide with the earliest possible time to call in.

Eligibility
Some people love to brag about all the tricks and ploys they use to snow ticket agents and airline counter personnel into parting with unearned upgrades. The system works best for those trav-

elers who have actually earned the right to sit up front through their elite status or through a purchased upgrade.

Show Some Class

In our experiences, sincerity and a reasonable attitude are the best routes to getting a better seat. Leave the groveling, grandstanding and theatrics to those who enjoy publicly embarrassing themselves. It is a small world after all, and the employee you bullied, badgered or battered into handing over today's upgrade may yet have the last laugh.

The key to asking for an upgrade is to request in a polite and non-offensive manner. Never demand. Gate agents say they are more likely to respond to a polite and direct request along the lines of, "If you are upgrading passengers on this flight, I would like to be considered."

When looking for that upgrade, dress your best. If you show up in nice clothes you are more likely to be upgraded than if you show up in ripped jeans (unless you are famous!).

Timing/Behavior

Know when to hang in (for example, if there is still a first class seat available) and when to graciously walk away. Sometimes the way you handle an initial rejection can actually up your chances at a later date.

Although carriers maintain a list of upgrade wannabes based on time of check-in, other factors come into play when the upgrades are actually allocated. Technically, the early bird may have first dibs on the worm, but a more senior member of a program can move up the list if he or she has professionally brought this factor to the attention of the list holder. Remember: When all else is equal, most folks opt to help the person who has made it easier—not harder—for them to do so.

Other Sources

Lacking the miles necessary for an upgrade? Look no further than your favorite hotel program. All major hotel programs offer members an option to redeem their points for miles. And since we have identified miles used for upgrade purposes often have a greater value than miles used for free flights, your hotel points just got more valuable.

Just Pay for the Darn Thing

Many times, tricks and tips simply are not worth the effort. If you absolutely, positively need more room, consider these options.

  1. Buy a business or first class ticket.

Because of the way the airline industry is repricing tickets, you might find that first class is within your reach. Whether booking through a travel agent, online or directly with the airline itself, it is strongly recommended to ask what the current fare for first class is. You might be surprised to hear what the cost is. Domestically, first class fares can be only $30 above that of discounted coach fares. Spend the money. And do not think the major airlines are the only ones with first class seating. Low cost carriers such as AirTran, America West, ATA and Sun Country offer alternatives to coach class with some of the very same services and space the large airlines offer. For example, upgrades to business class on AirTran are available in advance at the airport on the day of your flight, from just $35 to $75 over full coach fare (Y class) or from $70 to $120 on connecting flights. They are unfortunately not available for use with discounted fares. As well, ATA offers business class upgrades only at the gate and only payable by credit card. Prices vary by market and capacity on international routes.

Be sure to also watch for business class sales. Both British Airways and Continental are famous for springing for two day sales on business class tickets to Europe at or near $1,000 prices.

2. Buy a premium economy ticket.

A number of international airlines offer what is called "premium" economy seats. While not as good as business class (and the seats do not lower into beds), this section is good enough to qualify as comfortable even on a full flight. British Airways, bmi and Virgin Atlantic are among those that offer these seats from the United States to Europe; China Southern, EVA Air and Singapore Airlines all offer similar seating on flights to Asia. Pricing of these "upgrade" options vary from a few hundred dollars more than discounted coach to nearly another $1,000. On the low cost side this alternative is highly recommended. A few other airlines also claim premium economy seats but our experience has been that you need to ask around first because unless the seat is wider than the norm it is not going to be comfortable.

3. Buy a ticket for a good coach seat.

No, the term "good coach seat" is not an oxymoron. One small domestic line, Midwest, offers them on flights designated "Signature Service." Seating on DC9s and 717s is four abreast, and legroom, while still a bit tight, is better than what you will find on most other coach cabins. While prices are competitive with relatively unrestricted coach fares on major airlines, you are not likely to find any really low "sale" prices. The biggest problem is that Midwest is a very small airline serving about two dozen major U.S. cities from a primary hub in Milwaukee and a mini hub in Kansas City, thus flying Midwest Airlines might not be an option for you.

4. Buy a higher-priced coach ticket with an automatic upgrade.

Some major airlines offer no-cost, confirmed upgrades on higher-priced domestic coach tickets. In most cases, these upgrades are confined to connecting routes through the airlines' major hubs. If you need to buy an expensive coach ticket, it is a no-brainer. But if you had otherwise bought a much lower coach fare, the price premium to qualify for the upgrade could be substantial.

5. Buy two coach tickets.

Often, the cheapest way to assure lots of room is to buy two coach tickets. If your itinerary qualifies for a very low "sale" fare, two tickets at that price may well cost far less than any other upgrade approach. The numbers work out even better for two travelers on the same itinerary who can share one empty seat between them. However, you do not get extra legroom and you do not get any sort of premium cabin service. Most airlines allow you to buy two seats in a row, or three seats for two people, but you have to do it by phone to ensure seat assignments together. Note: When you buy two tickets most airlines will only give you frequent flyer miles for one of the seats. In their way of thinking, the other seat is not occupied and thus not eligible to earn miles.

6. Buy "twofer" business or first class tickets.

You can often get a "free" second (companion) ticket when you buy one business or first class ticket at full price. Various airlines often offer such twofers as short-term promotions. For year-round use, the Platinum American Express card provides twofers for intercontinental trips in business, first class or both on 20 airlines—Continental Airlines plus 19 foreign carriers. Carte Blanche (the premium option from Diners Club) provides twofers in premium economy, business and first class on British

Airways. United's new Avanti membership program provides twofers for business and first class flights from the United States to overseas destinations. Provided their itineraries are identical, twofers are great for two colleagues traveling together. They are obviously useless for individual travelers. If you are normally a coach traveler, keep in mind that even at half price, international business and first class bookings are far more expensive.

⊕ REMEMBER THIS:

- There are generally four types of upgrades: those comped to the highest elite members, those you redeem miles for, those you purchase as segment upgrades, and those you grovel for.

- If you have been inconvenienced by an airline do not hesitate to ask for an upgrade. It may be reason enough to upgrade you.

- When lacking miles for an upgrade, consider tapping your hotel points for the extra miles you may need.

Chapter 11

Using Airline Alliances

RAISE THE SUBJECT OF AIRLINE alliances in a group of travel savvy consumers and watch the sparks fly. The universe of frequent flyers divides roughly evenly between those who give alliances a thumbs up and those who think alliances are an empty promise or, worse, a sinister sleight of hand.

We cannot contest the fact that alliances have been good for airlines fortunate enough to qualify for membership. The cost savings and revenue increases are demonstrable and substantial.

But what are the real benefits to the traveling public?

Certainly the airlines themselves have been guilty of over-hyping alliance benefits to their customers, eliciting a healthy dose of skepticism from wary travelers.

The principal accusation of alliance detractors—that the cooperation among alliance partners is anti-competitive and inevitably leads to higher ticket prices—is a valid concern, albeit an as yet unsubstantiated one. The jury is still out on whether groups of airlines working together as alliances can charge more for tickets than airlines operating, and competing, independently.

Naysayers notwithstanding, we are in the camp that believes alliances are, on balance, positive for travelers and especially so for frequent flyer program participants.

Background: Where Alliances Came From

Close relationships between airlines are nothing new. For all the smash mouth competition among airlines, the industry operates within a highly cooperative framework. Airlines routinely sell and accept each other's tickets, transfer luggage between each other's flights and offer other conveniences. It always seems logical for non-competitive airlines to take that kind of cooperation to the next level, sharing codes, creating joint fares and participating in each other's frequent flyer programs. Airline alliances were just another step in that direction.

The history of airline alliances goes back to 1993 when Northwest and KLM were granted antitrust immunity to operate almost as a single carrier. They began by sharing codes on selected flights to the United States and to Europe, following that by integrating their mileage programs. By the end of the year, the two carriers were jointly operating all U.S. and European services. Some called it a virtual merger.

By whatever name, the tie-up was a financial success. In 1994, the first full year of operating cooperatively with KLM, Northwest posted a $295.5 million profit, the most of any U.S. carrier that year.

That outsized performance was attributed in large part to alliance-driven effects such as enhanced revenues and pared-down costs. These trends captured the attention of other large airlines, both in the United States and abroad, leading to the subsequent move toward more airline partner networks.

It was envisioned that the Northwest/KLM tie-up would expand to include Continental, Alitalia and others, and operate under the banner of Wings, a working name for the group. But Wings never fully materialized, and by 2004, Northwest, KLM, Continental and Alitalia had all signed on to the Delta led alliance, SkyTeam.

(Another alliance, Qualiflyer, which at one point included Air Europe, Air Littoral, AOM, Austrian, Crossair, Lauda Air, Swissair, Sabena, TAP Air Portugal, Turkish and Tyrolean, never truly reached global scale and was finally disbanded in 2003.)

The Promise of Alliances

Love 'em or loathe 'em, global alliances are a fact of travel life. By the end of 2005, approximately 80 percent of the world's airline seats will be offered by airlines participating in one of the three alliances: oneworld, SkyTeam and Star Alliance. (See the accompanying table on page 129 for profiles including participating airlines).

In each alliance, the member airlines work closely together in three broad areas, as follows.

Many Airlines, One Network

From a consumer standpoint, the main goal of the alliances is seamless worldwide travel. To that end, participating airlines have more or less integrated their flight routes, coordinating their schedules and flying from common terminals at shared hub airports so passengers connecting from one alliance partner to another can do so with minimal effort and inconvenience.

With an integrated route network in place, airlines in an alliance offer fares that favor a combination of alliance partners, including round-the-world fares that showcase the alliance's global network, permitting travelers to circumnavigate the earth exclusively using members of a single alliance. And the airlines link their mileage programs to reward travelers for flying within the alliance network.

What all this cooperation means to international flyers is a streamlined travel experience.

Following is a list of the key alliance consumer benefits and a note in parentheses on how they are obtained:

- Travelers can fly between hundreds of countries using a combination of alliance airlines (integrated route network).

- Travelers have the ability to buy a single competitively priced ticket (pricing coordination, marketing co-op).

- Because alliance partners share airport terminals, connections require no change of terminals (terminal co-location).

- If it is necessary to change planes en route, the connecting time will be short but adequate (coordinated schedules).

- Check in once on the outbound, once on the return. Each time, baggage is checked through to the final destination (terminal co-location, interline baggage coordination).

- Elite program members and first and business class passengers have access to lounge facilities at most airports (mileage program integration, lounge sharing).

◦ Travelers receive a uniform minimum standard of service and safety from alliance members (alliance-wide standards must be met by all participating members).

◦ Travelers enjoy expanded frequent flyer program benefits (enhanced multilateral program participation).

Frequent Flyer Program Integration

The core alliance "product" is a single global flight network cobbled together from the route systems of participating carriers. The key incentive when traveling with alliance partners is the link-up among the alliance carriers' frequent flyer programs.

For starters, every airline partner of each alliance is an earning and redemption partner in the mileage programs of every other member of the same alliance.

So, for example, a member of American's AAdvantage program can earn and redeem AAdvantage miles on the flights of all airlines participating in the oneworld alliance, of which American is a member. And members of the programs of all other oneworld airlines may earn and redeem miles for flights on American. (Note that American has partners in its program that are not members of the oneworld alliance including Alaska Airlines, El Al, Hawaiian and Japan Airlines. As you will see, miles earned for flights on alliance partners are more valuable than miles earned on non-alliance carriers, since the former count toward elite status and the latter do not.)

MEMORABLE MOMENTS
OF MILES 8 POINTS

OCTOBER 1992
Air Canada and United Airlines unveil an alliance agreement that becomes the cornerstone of the Star Alliance.

The alliance benefit goes beyond simply pumping up the

roster of earning and redemption partners of the alliance airlines' programs. To distinguish alliance partners from mere marketing partners, and to increase the cachet of the alliances themselves, special alliance-linked benefits are reserved for the most frequent travelers.

Elite Qualifying Miles on Alliance Partners

In a telling sign of the commitment to their respective alliances, member airlines award elite qualifying miles in their programs for flights on any and all alliance airline flights. This is significant alliance benefit and a powerful incentive for travelers to focus their travel on members of a single alliance.

For instance, rather than being restricted to flying Delta to earn elite qualifying miles, members of Delta's SkyMiles program can earn elite status by flying any SkyTeam airline, including Continental and Northwest.

Caveat: As one alliance Web site warns: "Accrual is subject to each airline's program rules. Some restrictions apply." In particular, program members should be aware of restrictions regarding "eligible fares." U.S. programs tend to award actual flown miles for both reward and elite qualification for most, if not all, published coach fares. When they launched their programs, many European and Asian carriers awarded only a portion of flown miles for discounted coach fares, or none at all, reasoning that low prices should be incentive enough. While there has been some movement to match U.S. carriers' more inclusive policy, fare restrictions remain in place at some airlines, which can trip up unwary consumers.

Alliance-Wide Elite Status and Perks

Based on the elite status a traveler has earned in a specific airline program, he or she is awarded separate elite status within the alliances. This entitles travelers to special benefits and recognition when they fly on any airline within the same alliance.

The qualification criteria and benefits vary by airline and alliance as follows:

oneworld

Elite members of oneworld airlines are awarded Ruby, Sapphire or Emerald status in the alliance, which entitles them to the following on all oneworld airlines:

- Ruby members receive priority check-in at business class counters, preferred seating, priority standby for whichever class of service they are booked in when flying on any oneworld airline.

- Sapphire members receive the same benefits as Ruby, plus access to business class airport lounges when international travel is involved.

- Emerald members receive Ruby benefits, plus access to first class airport lounges when international travel is involved.

oneworld status is awarded according to the status earned in the programs of participating airlines. For example, members of American's AAdvantage program who have earned Gold elite status receive Ruby status in oneworld while Platinum members earn Sapphire status and Platinum Executive members earn Emerald status.

Star Alliance

Star Alliance has two elite tiers: Silver and Gold.

- Silver members receive priority waitlisting on sold-out flights.

- Gold members receive Silver benefits plus priority airport check-in, priority baggage handling, extra baggage allowance, priority boarding and airport lounge access.

Members of United's loyalty program who have reached the two highest tiers in Mileage Plus, 1K or Premier Executive, automatically receive Gold status. Premier members of Mileage Plus are accorded Silver status.

Silver Preferred members of US Airways' Dividend Miles program earn Silver status; Gold Preferred and Chairman's Preferred members are given Gold status.

SkyTeam

SkyTeam has two elite tiers: Elite and Elite Plus.

- Elite members receive access to airport lounges when flying international first or business class, preferred seating, priority waitlist and standby, priority check-in and priority boarding.

- Elite Plus members receive Elite benefits plus access to airport lounges when flying on or connecting to/from an international flight operated by a SkyTeam carrier, priority baggage handling, and a guaranteed full-fare economy reservation even on sold-out long-haul flights (requires 24-hour notice).

Members of the programs of Continental, Delta and Northwest who have reached Silver or Gold status automatically receive Elite status. Platinum members of those programs receive Elite Plus status.

Cost Savings

While of little interest to consumers, airlines participating in alliances can realize significant cost savings by sharing facilities such as sales and ticket offices, by using their combined purchasing power to wrest volume discounts from suppliers of everything from jet fuel to in-flight meals, and by otherwise capitalizing on economies of scale realized through alliance participation.

In theory, those savings are ultimately passed along to all travelers by offering lower ticket prices.

The Payoff for (Some) Frequent Flyers

In the early stages of the alliances, benefits were limited to those traveling internationally. That is simply because the initial alliances never included more than one carrier from any single country.

That concept is still true for the oneworld alliance. An American AAdvantage member who lives in the United States and does not travel internationally will never earn elite qualifying miles on other oneworld carriers or otherwise benefit from the oneworld's global route network.

However, the situation has changed for the better at SkyTeam and Star.

Both alliances now have more than one U.S. airline partner. Continental, Delta and Northwest are all SkyTeam members.

Both United and US Airways participate in the Star Alliance. That means even domestic-only travelers can still receive significant added value from these groups. A member of United's Mileage Plus program, for instance, can earn elite qualifying miles for flying on US Airways. And having achieved elite status in the Star Alliance, he or she would be granted special recognition and benefits when traveling with US Airways.

Still, the biggest payoff from alliances is reserved for those travelers who regularly fly beyond the borders of their home countries. When everything works as advertised, flying on alliance partners is likely to be the quickest, most comfortable and hassle-free way of getting from point A to point B, short of a nonstop flight.

And from a miles and benefits standpoint, travel within the alliance networks can be uncommonly rewarding.

⊕ REMEMBER THIS:

- Global airline alliances are a fact of travel life. Use them to your benefit.

- Given a choice between an airline that participates in a global alliance and one that does not, choose the former. You will benefit from a world-wide network of flights when earning miles and when redeeming them for free flights.

- Familiarize yourself with the partners associated with your primary carrier's alliance. Use them whenever possible to earn elite qualifying miles.

Airline Alliances			
	oneworld	**SkyTeam**	**Star Alliance**
Launch Date	February 1, 1999	June 22, 2000	May 14, 1997
Partners	Aer Lingus American Airlines British Airways Cathay Pacific Finnair Iberia LAN Qantas	AeroMexico Air France Alitalia Continental CSA Czech Airlines Delta Air Lines KLM Korean Air Northwest	Air Canada Air New Zealand ANA Asiana Airlines Austrian bmi LOT Polish Airlines Lufthansa Scandinavian Airlines Singapore Airlines Spanair TAP Thai Airways United US Airways VARIG
Countries Served	129	133	139
Airports Served	588	684	795
Daily Departures	8,160	15,207	15,000
Fleet	1,998	2,069	2,554
Airport Lounges	392	391	620
Passengers Flown/Year (millions)	244.7	343.6	383.8
Web site	www.oneworld.com	www.skyteam.com	www.staralliance.com

Chapter 12

Identifying Optimum Awards

HOW DOES ONE GO ABOUT choosing the best awards from the thousands upon thousands of awards offered each year by all the assorted frequent travel programs?

As the old punch line goes: Very carefully (ba-da-boom).

In all likelihood, if you put 10 frequent travelers in a room and asked them to write down how they know they have received the best value for their award redemptions, most pages would be blank. The truth is that most members use awards just as they use cash and simply see award use as free transportation or a free hotel room and not as an exercise in money management. For most members, there is nothing wrong with that because the gratification of getting something for (nearly) free is still the best reward.

One thing we know is that awards have changed since the early days of loyalty programs. After 20-plus years of fine tuning, you generally are not going to find awards as lucrative as those offered in the early years when programs were more naive. But what you will find today are many, many more choices than what could be found in the 1980s. It is all about give and take.

Identifying the choicest awards is largely subjective. Do you prefer Hawaii or Europe? Is your idea of a perfect vacation an African safari or a relaxing cruise?

Setting aside personal preferences, some clear guidelines determine prime frequent flyer awards. The easiest way to value an award is against the cost of purchasing a similar ticket or itinerary. However, some awards (such as the Round-the-World award) comprise both a monetary value and the value of the actual experience. And then there are other awards—such as four nights in Egypt and a desert safari from InterContinental's Priority Club Rewards, or a one-night stay for two on the Club Level at any Ritz-Carlton worldwide from Diners Club Club Rewards. The latter offer high "experience" value as related to cost.

Our recommendation for discovering your choice award is to look through the descriptions of the various airline and hotel programs until you find the award that fits your particular needs and desires. As you will see, some awards are designed for families or groups, while others offer lower award thresholds for seat upgrades. Still, others offer exotic trips to foreign locations via partnerships with foreign carriers.

We suggest that you set a goal and then utilize all the tips and information contained in this book to reach that goal as rapidly and easily as possible. Following are some basic tips:

- Be mindful of restrictions such as blackout dates and capacity controls. An award with blackout dates may be of significantly less value than a similar award without such restrictions.

♦ Examine award descriptions with great care and
thoughtfulness. A one- or even two-level upgrade in
a rental car is relatively worthless when compared to
a free week's rental. Likewise, there is a big difference
between a 25 percent hotel discount (off what rate?)
and three free days upgraded to the club floor or the
best available room.

♦ Once you have established a goal, learn all the ways
to enhance point accumulation for that award. For
example, know the ins and outs of hotel, car rental
and affinity credit card partnerships. Keep your eyes
peeled for bonuses and promotions that require regis-
trations. And, of course, continue to "top off" any secondary accounts you may have. (Reminder: Affinity
credit card use often offers worlds of opportunities.)

♦ Pay attention to special seasonal offers such as "fly
six segments between X and Y dates and qualify for
a free companion ticket." These are often exceptional
values when you already need to travel to these
destinations or can adjust optional travel to meet
the special date restriction.

While all major airlines offer every single seat on a flight for
award redemption, keep in mind that most programs offer
discounted awards that require fewer miles for redemption but
are subject to capacity controls through which the number of
available seats for award travel is limited. It is important to plan
as far in advance as possible when it comes to these awards.
(Securing awards at least six months in advance of your travel is
recommended, especially if your trip closely coincides with a

blackout period. And paying for award redemption assistance is sometimes warranted.) Note: All major programs offer two types of award redemptions: Any Time and Saver. Any Time means just that: Any time a seat is available for sale it is also available for award redemption. Granted these awards cost more miles, but nonetheless, it does mean you can plan on going somewhere. Saver awards are the more popular 25,000-mile awards and often have restrictions by flight and date. Some flights may not have any seats at this reward level, while others may have 20 or 30 seats. It all depends on the destination, time of flight and the demand from other loyalty program members.

For many travelers, the award that offers the single best value is the "typical" 25,000-mile unrestricted or semi-restricted coach ticket. This award has allowed thousands upon thousands of small business owners and people who work for small companies to make business trips on short notice, without a mandatory Saturday night stay except with programs that limit its use such as Continental OnePass and Northwest WorldPerks.

Consider this: A midweek business trip often runs anywhere from $600 to $1000 or more (or about 25,000 reward miles), while a pre-planned, stay-over-Saturday-night trip to Hawaii or Europe has about the same dollar value, yet will cost you three to four times as many miles.

Optimum Value

When it comes to getting the absolute biggest bang for your buck, optimum awards are generally upgrades to business class using a purchased economy ticket topped off by frequent flyer miles. Depending on the program, this investment of 10,000 to 40,000 miles can be worth $4,000 or more. What is more, business class on almost every airline in the world these days is so superior to what first class was just five years ago that it does not make sense to redeem the extra 35,000 to 75,000 additional miles it would take to ride all the way up front. Here is an example: Members of the American AAdvantage program can fly from Chicago to Honolulu (about eight or nine hours each way) in coach for about $850. They could redeem 15,000 miles each way to upgrade to business class (30,000 miles total). The current price of a business class ticket is $4,976. The savings of more than $4,000 is just part of it. The member will earn about 8,500 miles from the paid flight, which means the upgrade only cost 21,500 miles, and the best part is that you were not cooped up in coach.

> MEMORABLE MOMENTS
> OF MILES & POINTS
>
> **FEBRUARY 1995**
>
> All major programs increased their "saver" domestic awards from 20,000 miles to 25,000 miles effective February 1, 1995. Alaska Mileage Plan increased their comparable award from 15,000 miles to 20,000 miles. These capacity-controlled awards are by far the most popular award for redemption among U.S. programs.

Some members will be keen on "tailor made" awards such as those possible through Diners Club Club Rewards and InterContinental Hotels Group Priority Club. For instance, if a traveler earns more than 100,000 points in the Diners Club program, he or she can draw up a personalized itinerary or award and Diners Club will then determine a point value for the award. These awards range from trips to the Arctic to highly prized country club memberships and even braces for your kid's teeth. These types of awards are not necessarily the richest when compared to the optimum use of miles and points, but they often have an aspirational value that far exceeds any clearly determined monetary value.

We will stop short of analyzing "what is a mile worth," since that topic is addressed in the next chapter on converting miles and points in money.

⊕ REMEMBER THIS:

- Identifying the best awards is largely subjective. Is your idea of a perfect vacation an African safari or a relaxing cruise? The easiest way to value an award is against the cost of purchasing a similar ticket or itinerary.

- Most members use awards just as they use cash; it is something for free, not an exercise in money management.

- The absolute biggest bang for your buck is to use miles to upgrade internationally to business class when purchasing an economy ticket.

Chapter 13

Converting Miles and Points into Money

AIRLINE LOYALTY PROGRAMS HAVE PROVEN themselves to be uncommonly powerful. That power derives from two sources: one purely emotional (the aspirational value of travel) and the other more quantifiable (the actual dollar value of travel).

As a reward, nothing packs quite the aspirational punch that travel does. In the real world of security lines, oversold flights and a weak U.S. dollar, a trip away from home is still an enticement without any equal. That is because a trip-to-be is a fantasy. It is a repository of hopes and dreams. It is also an escape into mystery, into romance, into adventure. It is a getaway packed with invaluable memories. But it does come with a price.

The Dollars and Cents of Miles

There are ways to put a price tag on miles.

Miles have different values when observed from different

perspectives: when they are accumulated, when they are redeemed, and how they are viewed by the airlines' own accountants. (One reason the IRS has stopped short of taxing frequent flyer miles is that there is no simple, straightforward way to assign a value to those miles—a prerequisite to computing tax liability.)

Want Miles with That?

How much does it cost to earn a frequent flyer mile? Answer(s): nothing, something or it depends.

In one sense, frequent flyer miles are free. For your next airline flight or hotel stay, price your airline ticket or hotel booking both with earning and without earning frequent flyer miles. The cost of the ticket or hotel stay will be the same either way. So, in the great majority of cases, there is no extra cost for earning miles. They are free.

(The flip side of this is that you are, in effect, overpaying if you decline to earn miles for a transaction for which miles are offered. It would be like telling the dealer to keep the spare tire even though it is included in the car's price. By doing that, you would be receiving less than full dollar value.)

MEMORABLE MOMENTS OF
MILES & POINTS

AUGUST 1986

American AAdvantage and TWA Frequent Flight Bonus sue frequent flyer coupon brokers, citing that awards are being transferred to family members.

In another sense, frequent flyer miles cannot be free. Participating companies spend money to operate their loyalty programs by employing customer service reps, by establishing call centers, and by funding marketing communications. Like all operating costs, those expenses are folded into the price of the product and then passed along to customers. When you buy an airline ticket, the cost of frequent flyer miles is included in the price whether you choose to earn the miles or not.

There are cases where the purchase price with and without miles varies depending on where the purchase is made. As an example, mileage earners routinely face a choice between earning miles when purchasing from an online retailer linked to one of the airline's mileage malls or when purchasing the same item for less at a competing retailer that does not award miles. So, which is it? Earn the miles or get the lower price?

The first step in making an informed decision is to compute the cost of the miles. Divide the price difference (which is the difference between the price with miles and the discounted price without miles) by the number of miles awarded for the purchase to arrive at the price per mile. Then ask yourself whether you will be able to recoup the cost of the miles when they are redeemed.

So, in the hypothetical case of a Sony Walkman purchased for $100 earning two airline miles for every dollar spent versus buying the same item elsewhere for $80 but without the benefit of earning miles, you would pay an extra $20 to earn 200 miles. That is 10 cents per mile.

As we have established elsewhere in this chapter, the average value of a frequent flyer mile is somewhat less than two cents. So paying 10 cents per mile is a stretch. In this case, the financially prudent decision would be to buy the cheaper Walkman and forego the miles.

Redemption Value

For most loyalty program members, where the rubber meets

the road is on the award side of the programs. What can I get for my miles? How much is that award worth?

Assuming the award is a free ticket its value is simply the price of a comparable paid ticket in the marketplace. And the value of the individual miles is the price of that revenue ticket divided by the number of miles redeemed.

So, if a restricted coach ticket between Philadelphia and San Francisco can be had either by redeeming 25,000 miles or by paying $391, you would be getting about 1.6 cents per mile if you elected to use miles for the flight ($391÷25,000 miles).

If cheaper flights were available, the value of the miles would be lower. If the flights were more expensive, the miles would yield a higher value.

Recognizing and capitalizing on this value variability is key to maximizing mileage payoff. The general rule: To get the most bang for your buck, cash in your miles for more expensive flights. Or to put this rule in the form of a caveat: Do not redeem your hard earned miles for a ticket you could have purchased for a paltry $99.

Comparing award tickets and revenue tickets is a bit over-simplified. In particular, frequent flyer awards—at least restricted awards that are requested the great majority of the time—are subject to much stricter capacity controls than revenue tickets. That restricted availability arguably diminishes their value by increasing the hassle factor in obtaining them. Other factors undermining the value of award tickets versus revenue tickets: Award trips do not earn miles and award travel cannot be upgraded.

While it may be an imperfect approximation, comparing an award ticket to a comparable revenue ticket remains a simple and reliable way to benchmark the value of redeemed miles. It is a computation that loyalty program members should make every time they consider cashing in their miles for an award.

Buy 12 Get 1 Free

Another way to place a value on frequent flyer earnings is to think in terms of the number of paid trips required to earn a free trip.

This approach lends itself especially well to some of the discount airlines' loyalty schemes that offer a free ticket after a set number of paid tickets are acquired.

The obvious example is Southwest. This airline offers members of its Rapid Rewards program a free roundtrip ticket after eight paid roundtrips. The value proposition is very straightforward: Fly eight times and get the ninth flight free. Rather than looking for a dollar value, this highlights the discount or rebate aspect of frequent flyer awards. In Southwest's case, the member who fully participates, making the required eight paid trips within 24 months and then taking the free award trip, effectively gets an 11 percent rebate.

Miles and Points for Sale

Travel loyalty programs sell their miles and points to two distinct sets of customers: Individual travelers who are members of their programs, and companies that participate in the programs as partners by purchasing miles from the program operators and using them to reward customers for buying their products or services.

Compared to the sale of miles to program partners, which goes back to the programs' earliest days, selling miles directly to the traveling public is a recent development.

When purchased by individual travelers directly from the airlines, miles can cost as much as 5.5 cents apiece when purchased

The Two Cent Myth

Anyone seeking frequent flyer program wisdom will eventually discover the myth of the Two Cent Rule.

This rule addresses the question at the top of any enlightened frequent flyer's list: How much is a frequent flyer mile worth?

The answer (drum roll, please): Two cents.

As a generalization, that is just plain wrong, which is why we call it a myth.

In its day, though, it was a fairly reliable rule of thumb. That is because it proceeded from a sound premise: That the value of a mile was related to the price of a revenue ticket.

So, based on the average cost to purchase a domestic roundtrip ticket (around $400) and the number of frequent flyer miles required for a comparable award ticket (20,000 in most programs), the value of a frequent flyer mile was indeed two cents ($400÷20,000). That was then.

In the years since the rule was formulated, the values of both key variables have changed. In 1995, most programs increased the number of miles required for a restricted coach award from 20,000 to 25,000 miles. And, due largely to the pricing pressures exerted by the low cost carriers, the average price of a paid coach ticket has decreased from around $400 to about $300.

Replacing the outdated variables with current ones, the formula generates a current average mile value of 1.2 cents. However, factoring in the difficulty of obtaining award seats and other negatives, the final value is closer to one cent.

Although the original conclusion is no longer accurate, the approach remains valid. And while your mileage may vary, the average value of a frequent flyer mile currently stands at about a penny.

in small quantities, but are usually priced at around 2.8 cents each, including processing fees and a 7.5 percent Federal Excise Tax. All airlines impose a cap on the number of miles travelers can purchase, ranging from 7,500 to 40,000 miles per calendar year.

To put the per mile price into perspective, purchasing enough miles to cash in for a free restricted domestic coach ticket (25,000 in most programs) at 2.8 cents per mile would cost $700. That amount is far more than an advance purchase ticket would cost on the open market. And a revenue ticket would not be encumbered by the capacity controls of the award ticket.

Where purchasing miles may make economic sense is in situations where a small number of miles are needed to reach an award threshold. If, for example, you were just 1,000 miles short of the 25,000 required for a free domestic ticket, purchasing those miles for $28.00 to "top off" the account would be a quick and easy solution.

As you might expect, airlines that sell miles to other companies do so in larger quantities and at lower prices.

Where a maximum number of miles are available for purchase by individuals, there are a minimum number of miles for companies wishing to use them to reward their own employees or, more often, their customers. That minimum is generally 200,000 miles.

For lesser quantities, airlines charge companies approximately 2.5 cents per mile. When the quantities increase, volume pricing can drive the per mile price down below 1.5 cents.

So, combining the purchase price of airline miles to individual travelers and to both smaller and larger partner companies, the average per mile price is in the neighborhood of two cents. (The airlines do not disclose this level of detail in their financial reports, thus it is impossible to be precise.)

You Won... A Tax Liability

Another data point: The airline must assign frequent flyer miles given away in contests and sweepstakes a dollar value in order to report the winner's tax liability to the IRS. (Yes, there is an apparent disconnect between how the IRS treats miles earned and how the IRS treats miles won in sweepstakes.)

In the terms and conditions of sweepstakes, the ARV (approximate retail value) of miles awarded as prizes ranges from 2 to 2.5 cents. So, if you win a million frequent flyer miles, be prepared to be taxed on $20,000 of additional income. That would increase the average taxpayer's IRS bill by about $6,000.

Pssst... Wanna Sell Those Miles?

Finally, like anything of value, miles and points can be bought and sold. The bad news is that all airline and hotel programs explicitly prohibit such sales, except through authorized channels as discussed above.

The following legal verbiage quoted (and edited for clarity) from the terms and conditions of American's AAdvantage program is typical:

> *At no time may AAdvantage mileage credit or award tickets be purchased, sold or bartered. Any such mileage or tickets are void if transferred for cash or other consideration. Violators (including any passenger who uses a purchased or bartered award ticket) may be liable for damages and litigation costs,*

*including American Airlines' attorneys fees incurred
in enforcing this rule.*

Use of award tickets that have been acquired by purchase or
for any other consideration may result in the tickets being confiscated or the passenger being denied boarding. If a trip has been
started, any continued travel will be at the passenger's expense
on a full-fare basis. The passenger and member may also be liable
to American Airlines for the cost of a full-fare ticket for any segments flown on a sold or bartered ticket.

Although against the programs' rules, a fairly active market
in selling and purchasing miles thrives, both directly between
buyers and sellers and via coupon brokers. The latter match-
maker of would-be buyers and sellers charges a commission for
their services. (To get a sense of the scale of such activity, simply
run a Google or other Internet browser keyword search for "frequent flyer miles.")

Many frequent travelers are outraged by the airlines' restrictions on the use of miles, reasoning that having earned the miles
legitimately they are the traveler's property to use as he or she
sees fit.

From the airlines' standpoint, the sale of miles—or more
accurately, the sale of award tickets since the miles themselves
cannot be transferred—amounts to a gray market for their
product that undermines the published prices available through
authorized sales channels and ultimately depresses profits.

No matter which side of the argument you choose to subscribe
to, we suggest that you strictly observe the airlines' policies.

First and foremost, doing otherwise is against the rules. Secondly, it is not worth the risk and anxiety to make or save a few
dollars. At the very least, those caught selling their miles will

have their accounts frozen, forfeiting any remaining miles. (It is up to the airline to reopen the member's account or to close it permanently.) And buyers who are detected will have their tickets confiscated when checking in for their flights.

⊕ **REMEMBER THIS:**

- On average, the value of a frequent flyer mile is approximately one cent.

- By redeeming miles for expensive tickets and upgrades, savvy travelers can get significantly more value from their miles.

- Caveat: Do not overpay to earn miles. In some cases, you are better off buying a cheaper product and foregoing miles. Do the math.

Chapter 14

The Fine Print: Legal and Taxation Issues

SOME OFFICIAL ESTIMATES CURRENTLY PUT the number of lawyers in the United States at about one million. That is approximately one attorney for every three hundred people. With this in mind, do not be surprised to learn that there are some legal issues attached to your miles and points.

Since the beginning of the contemporary frequent flyer program, more than a few spats between programs and members have landed in front of a judge. For example, the infamous case of Wolens v. American Airlines AAdvantage that went all the way to the U.S. Supreme Court before being sent back down for resolution in Chicago's circuit court. In this case, plaintiffs challenged retroactive changes in AAdvantage's terms and conditions, including American's imposition of capacity controls (limits on seats available to passengers obtaining tickets with frequent flyer miles) and blackout dates (restrictions on dates when miles could be used). Fortunately, these types of lawsuits are not the norm. The typical traveler will only run into frequent flyer related legal issues in three unfortunate instances: death, taxes and divorce.

Taxes

The topic of taxing frequent flyer awards is as old as the programs themselves. Although they may feel like freebies, frequent flyer awards are not since they are earned through purchased flights and hotel stays, as well as a myriad of merchandise purchases— so, when taxes creep into the picture, the good feeling of getting free flights and hotel stays is seriously diminished. Like a bad penny, the issue always continues to surface.

For now, you are safe. In February 2002, the IRS clarified once and for all that frequent flyer miles earned from business travel would not be taxed as income.

This news ended more than a decade of ambiguity about whether or not the IRS might spring the value of employer-paid frequent flyer miles on unsuspecting taxpayers in an audit. The taxation topic was kicked around for a few years without an official ruling until 1988, when, without explanation, the IRS suspended consideration of the plan to tax frequent flyer benefits. Speculations were that, after two years of looking for ways to tax miles and awards, the IRS decided that administering such an effort would not be worth the cost.

In 1993, a private IRS ruling indicated that frequent flyer miles earned through employer-paid business travel might be viewed as a taxable fringe benefit. Award miles earned in personal travel, or by partner use such as credit cards, were deemed untaxable. Because the IRS provided no further guidance on valuing mileage or reporting it to the government, that ruling and subsequent ones were widely ignored.

In 1997, the Taxpayer Relief Act was quietly passed. As part of this act, when a program member receives miles from one of the airline's partners (such as a hotel or car rental company) the partner must purchase the miles from the sponsoring airline with a 7.5 percent tax placed on top of the purchase. For example, if Hilton rewards you with miles for staying with them, the hotel company must buy those miles from the airline (in order to give them to you) and must also pay the 7.5 percent on top of the purchase price.

What does the tax mean to the frequent flyer? In all probability, the cost is passed on to the consumer/frequent flyer in the form of fees. According to the travel industry, partners' profit margins for these miles are so slim that the tax cost would wipe out the partners. Still, they need to partner with the airlines to keep their market share. So, the partners remain in the frequent flyer program business and the costs are passed onto the consumer—that is you!

In the subsequent three years, the tax has appeared to consumers in the form of:

- Fewer miles awarded when a cheaper ticket is purchased.

- Greater mileage requirements for tickets (for example, raising the number of miles needed for a free coach ticket).

- Transaction fees for redemption of mileage awards.

Car rental companies were the first to respond publicly to the increase in price. National Car Rental announced that it would not directly pass along the tax cost to consumers; however, the car company did reduce the amount of miles awarded for selected rentals. Hertz and Avis followed suit, reducing the number of miles awarded for selected rentals from 500 per day to 250 miles, and now to the current award of 50 miles. Unfortunately, this is how car rental companies solved their tax dilemma. It could have been worse for frequent flyers. In 1998, many car rental companies considered reducing the number of airline frequent flyer programs in which they participated. This would have been detrimental to the average business traveler who is often forced to rent vehicles to shuttle from meeting to meeting.

In mid 2000, Hertz began to blatantly pass the taxes onto travelers by requiring frequent flyer awards be subjected to a 50-cent transaction tax recovery fee.

Other frequent flyer program partners also pass the buck when it comes to frequent flyer taxes. MCI WorldCom and Sprint both add the tax to regular monthly phone bills. Interestingly, some partners, such as giant Hilton HHonors, have not passed this tax onto their customers. Somehow HHonors manages to award both points and miles through its revolutionary Double Dip program without needing to pass the tax onto customers.

FUN HISTORICAL FACT: In 1988, General Rent-A-Car held a promotion of 3,000 miles per rental. To take advantage of this generous offer, travelers would rent a car, drive it around the airport for a few minutes, and return it. They would then immediately rent another car, get another 3,000 miles, and return the car shortly thereafter. They did this seven more times and walked away with 27,000 miles. In Florida, you could rent a car from General Rent-A-Car for $9.99 day, so for $90 (9 x $9.99) you got a free plane ticket (25,000 miles with 2,000 to spare).

Death

Nearly all major North American programs offer some means of transferring the miles of the dearly departed. But, as you might expect, those means vary significantly. Fees, documentation, even requirements as to whether or not the miles were specifically referenced in a will, vary by airline.

Despite the variations in methods, though, there are almost always ways to get the transfers done, and in most cases, survivors have been pleased by the airlines' efforts.

Take the case of Arlene H. of New York City who was widowed in 2003.

She and her husband both had accounts with a number of airlines: America West, American, British Airways and Delta. Her husband had a considerable sum of miles built up—somewhere in the neighborhood of 200,000.

When the time came, she went to work, calling each of the airlines and requesting the miles be transferred to her.

> MEMORABLE MOMENTS
> OF MILES & POINTS
>
> **APRIL 1986**
> **In Southmark v. United Airlines**
> (Supreme Court, N.Y. County 1986) Southmark brought a class-action suit against seven major airlines attempting to force the airlines to permit the transfer of frequent flyer mileage to employers. The court dismissed the complaint for failure to state a cause of action. In other words, the court held that the airlines were not required to provide an employer with employee account information detailing miles and benefits earned by the employee through frequent flyer programs.

"American charged $50, but there was no problem. They were just great," she said. "And Delta was fine."

Few programs in the United States allow mileage pooling—that is, the ability for two members to effectively share their accounts. British Airways does, which makes things much easier for survivors. "With British Airways, we had a family account, and I just notified them that [my husband] had passed away. They converted the account to my name," Arlene said.

Other program members, while generally pleased with the results of their transfer efforts, have started to run into another obstacle: processing fees.

Not all airlines require a fee, and many will waive it under the right circumstances, but the $50-plus fees charged by some programs are simply too high for some members.

Carolyn V. of Chicago faced the fee quandary while in the process of transferring her deceased father's United Mileage Plus miles into her mother's account. With Mileage Plus, that transfer required $75.

"I am paying the fee but protesting," she said at the time. "They should take into consideration that she is an 82-year-old widow on a fixed income and that $75 is too high in her circumstances."

In Carolyn's case, her father's account had about 25,000 miles—not a mileage fortune, but enough for a free domestic ticket. With larger accounts—accounts that hold hundreds of thousands if not millions of miles, a double digit fee might seem more reasonable.

Fees aside, there are a few steps individuals can take to smooth out the transfer process.

First and foremost, accurate and accessible record keeping is a must. Arlene H. understands the importance of detail, particularly after her own experience. "I am very cautious. I want my kids to have those miles, so I keep very clear records."

When planning their estates, members should list their miles in a will, specifying how they would like them to be dispersed.

Also, it is best to name just one beneficiary. When programs allow the transfer of miles or points, they may well be bending their own rules. The chance for success is much higher and the process is easier if there is only one party to whom the transfer can be made.

In some cases, the difference between a single beneficiary and multiple beneficiaries can mean the difference between keeping miles active or being forced to redeem them immediately should one of the beneficiaries want free travel right away.

According to United, for example, "If there are multiple beneficiaries, the mileage will be transferred into the account of the executor or personal representative of the estate, and they will assume responsibility for ordering award certificates for the beneficiaries." We should note that the executor, or personal representative, is not required to redeem the miles right away. The account is treated like any other, requiring activity in the account (usually about every three years) to keep the miles from expiring.

> Issuing tickets from a deceased person's frequent flyer account is a popular way to bequeath awards to charitable organizations.

Not surprisingly, because of all the complications and fees involved in the transfer of miles upon death, many people simply assume the role of the deceased for the purpose of cashing in awards. Often a survivor will have access to the deceased passenger's frequent flyer number and PIN and will just use the remaining miles to issue tickets in whatever name they see fit. This is a popular method used to bequeath awards to charitable organizations.

This is, of course, against the rules. All airlines make a specific point in their terms and conditions that accounts belong solely to an individual, and that any attempt to "infiltrate" that member's account by another party is taboo.

The obvious response is: "How are they going to catch me?"

They may not. We are not aware of any cases in which an "identity assumer" has been nabbed. But the fact remains that this approach runs contrary to the spirit of the programs, and since there are "lawful" means of transferring these miles, the risks involved may not be worth it.

The Legal Fine Print of Death

Some elect to include a codicil (an addendum) to an existing last will and testament, though this often requires the assistance of an attorney. An easier solution might be to include this sample paragraph along with your will or, if no will is intended, this paragraph could be used if it is signed, dated and witnessed and kept with your personal papers:

"Upon my death I leave all my airline and hotel frequent flyer miles and/or points in my accounts to my (relationship), (name)."

The use of this paragraph will leave no question as to your wishes for your miles and points. While these same programs are constantly changing their rules with regard to leaving miles to heirs and beneficiaries, we advise you to check with your programs in advance before planning a specific action regarding your miles. And when doing so, it is probably best to remain anonymous when asking the question.

Divorce

As with wills, divorce laws vary considerably by state. There is no single rule of thumb regarding the disposition of miles.

As a general rule, any interest that may be considered "property" is subject to division, and therein lies the rub: Are frequent flyer miles property?

As of yet, no court has been willing to make that declaration. Two cases on record, one in Colorado and one in Florida, have treated miles as a marital asset without specifically declaring them property. In two other cases, one in New Mexico and one in Tennessee, the courts have divided miles between parties, a division that was not questioned on appeal.

Yet in Washington, in 1999, an appellate court specifically declared miles to be deemed separate property, thus avoiding the division question entirely.

One of the keys to determining whether or not something constitutes property is the concept of transferability. Rarely will a property interest be found if the owner cannot transfer one asset to another.

In some cases, the courts have left it at this: Since, under the rules of most programs, transfers are not allowed, no property interest exists. However, a few clever attorneys have suggested that miles are indeed transferable, regardless of what the rules say. There is, after all, an active black market in mile brokerage, with a number of Web sites devoted to that purpose.

"A lively market for the sale, exchange and barter of (miles) has existed for a number of years," attorney Barry Roberts explains. "(Members) consider their mileage credits to be an asset that can be sold, bartered or exchanged in a free market

MEMORABLE MOMENTS OF MILES & POINTS

NOVEMBER 1986

The first consumer lawsuit involving a member of a frequent flyer program: **Howard Landau vs. United Airlines. Dubbed "the man who flew too much" by** *The New York Times,* Howard Landau sued United on November 8, 1986 in the United States District Court of New Jersey. United had confiscated Mr. Landau's Mileage Plus accounts and those of his immediate family because (1) he had family members fly in his name, and (2) he sold mileage to a coupon broker. Arguing there were no rules prohibiting these actions at the time he enrolled in the Mileage Plus program, Mr. Landau sought reinstatement of his earned mileage and/or compensatory damages. United's motion for summary judgment was denied by Judge Maryann Trump-Barry (Donald Trump's sister) in an opinion that included the following observation: "Plaintiff's (Landau's) affidavits set forth numerous facts, uncontroverted by the defendant (United), that United unilaterally changed the rules of the game to frustrate coupon brokers and the Howard Landaus of the world. Because of the defendant's status as a powerful monolithic corporation, its ability to unilaterally alter the terms of consumer contracts is subject to the scrutiny traditionally afforded contracts of adhesion and other concepts derived from the potentially unequal bargaining position of consumers." United settled with Howard Landau. Terms of the settlement were not disclosed by mutual agreement of the parties. However, it is known that, subsequent to the settlement, Mr. Landau continued to sell mileage from his very significant mileage arsenal.

just like any other asset."

The drawback to this argument is that a black market does not necessarily constitute an "open" market. A court would probably be reluctant to attach a value to a commodity—in this case, miles—when the only means of determining that value is illegitimate.

Nevertheless, a divorcing spouse can try to make the case. If a valid third-party estimate of the value of miles can be attained, the court would likely consider a division.

The problem is that establishing a value is tricky at best. Three cases, one in Florida and two in Virginia, simply rejected a monetary award in lieu of miles because no evidence of value had been presented. Legal experts suggest that evidence is unlikely to arise anytime soon. Brett R. Turner, the author of numerous articles on this subject, says, "It is probably not possible to value frequent flyer miles with sufficient accuracy to permit an offsetting award."

Some courts have indeed placed a value on miles, using the familiar "two cent" rule (the cost of a domestic ticket, $500, divided by the number of miles required to earn that ticket, 25,000).

> MEMORABLE MOMENTS
> OF MILES & POINTS
>
> **FEBRUARY 2002**
>
> The IRS issued a formal policy clarifying its position that frequent flyer miles earned from business travel will not be taxed as income.

Of course, that assumes the "two cent" valuation is valid. However, as most frequent flyers know, this is not always the best way to estimate value. Two individuals, given the same number of miles in the same program can come up with a variety of award options, some of which are clearly more valuable than others. Value is entirely subjective.

In the absence of any clear and fair way to value frequent flyer miles, some have suggested the only equitable means of division is to simply split the miles. But, the airline and hotels may not be willing to play along. In the absence of a court

THE FINE PRINT: LEGAL AND TAXATION ISSUES

order, not every program will set up a new account. Take these unambiguous words from the Hilton HHonors terms and conditions: "Accrued points do not constitute the property of the member, and are not transferable in the event of death, divorce or operation of law."

In that case, the division needs to be done "indirectly"—that is, strictly between the parties. Under a written agreement, the mileage owner will, over time, dole out awards in the other party's name.

HHonors would not need to know about this agreement as it is between the two parties with the lawyer often assisting in making the agreement "stick." While the agreement could be given to HHonors to prove, one must still be wary of HHonors' "rules."

In the case of a hostile divorce, such a division is unlikely. In a more amicable situation, however, and with the help of good record keeping, such splits have been and continue to be made.

Solutions are really only as limited as the willingness of the parties.

Consider the case of Bob S. from Salt Lake City, Utah.

Prior to his divorce, Bob had been a prolific mile collector. Not surprisingly, his abundant bank of miles and points came up during his divorce. Faced with valuation difficulties, both sides came up with a novel plan.

"What we finally settled on, and this is actually in the written agreement, is that I had to give her enough points for a week in the Caribbean with Hilton," Bob said.

"Hilton required a copy of the divorce agreement, then split the points into two accounts, and transferred the points over. [Hilton was] very efficient; they just assigned a new account number. It was really a piece of cake."

The amicability of Bob's divorce may not have been the norm, but the creative use of his points has helped maintain a civil post-marital relationship. Since the split, he has voluntarily used his mileage bank to send his "ex" and their children on vacations.

"Let's face it," he says, "you can buy some good will. It is basically free, and can benefit the kids, and it is certainly a good way to negotiate."

Other Considerations

All this talk of "assets," "rights" and "valuation" begs the question: Whose miles are they anyway?

The fact is that even though members often believe their miles are individual property, the programs' terms and conditions are quite clear: The miles are an intangible currency that belongs solely to the program.

Of course, a good case can possibly be made that a property right does exist. Take the case of a few Delta flyers whose miles were confiscated by the program for violations of program rules. Their attorney quite specifically called those miles a property right, and it did not hurt his case that in events of death and divorce, the airlines treat them as such. The case is still in litigation.

But there is danger here.

As it stands, the IRS has said it has no interest in pursuing the taxation of miles at this time. If, however, the courts begin to create clear rules about the valuation of miles, it is not unforeseeable that this newfound property could be taxed.

Furthermore, when an airline offers to transfer miles in the case of death or divorce, they are, in essence, doing their customer a favor. If push comes to shove, it is plausible that they could alter their rules to keep their liability low.

Which in turn illustrates the most important point of all (and one veteran flyers know all too well): You can catch more flies with honey than with vinegar.

Your approach, and your value to the program, can make all the difference. Airlines and hotels have rules, and when cornered, will happily roll out all the fine print you could ever want. "Policies," on the other hand, tend to be a little more flexible.

⊕ REMEMBER THIS:

- ⟡ In 2002, the IRS finally declared that frequent flyer miles earned from business travel would not be taxed as income.

- ⟡ Donating miles to a charity is not tax deductible.

- ⟡ While members believe that their miles and points belong to them, the truth is that they are an intangible currency belonging solely to the loyalty program.

Chapter 15

Expiring Miles and Points

LOVE MAY BE ETERNAL. MILES and points are not.

When American's AAdvantage program launched in 1981, members' miles expired after 12 months. Two weeks later, when United countered with its own program, Mileage Plus, there was no termination date imposed on the miles—one of several "Plus" benefits United hoped would differentiate their program from archrival American's.

Since then, travelers have been subjected to an ever-changing patchwork of policies ranging from miles that lasted forever to miles that automatically disappeared after just one year.

After the long period of experimentation, the largest airlines settled on a mileage expiration approach that split the considerable difference between American's initial draconian use-'em-or-lose-'em policy and Continental's and Delta's eternal miles. Let's call it the Rolling Three-Year Rule:

> Miles do not expire as long as there is some account
> activity—either earning or redemption—every
> three years. Or, to put it differently: The life of all
> miles in an account is extended by three years from
> the date of any account activity.

That policy began taking shape in 1988 when United imposed a three-year lifespan (no extensions) on miles in its program. In 1995, Delta was the first major carrier to introduce a version of the current three-year rule, which links the life of miles to account activity. But initially only Delta or Delta Connection flights triggered an extra three years of life for banked miles.

It was not until 1999 that an industrywide move toward the current version of the three-year rule took place. It was led by Northwest, which in March of that year announced that, henceforth, any earning activity in a WorldPerks member's account would extend the life of all miles for 36 months.

So, how many miles ultimately do expire? Industry analysts estimate that over the long term, between 20 and 30 percent of all earned miles are lost to expiration.

So, essentially, you could have your miles forever as long as you have some form of activity every three years.

An AAdvantage member could protect his or her miles simply by engaging in any of the following transactions once every three years: Flying on American Airlines, American Eagle and more than 20 other airlines participating in the AAdvantage program (which includes airlines in the oneworld alliance), or earning miles with participating hotel companies, car rental firms, the

Citibank AAdvantage credit card and hundreds of other partner companies offering AAdvantage miles.

United, always responsive to American's moves, took the concept one step further, revising its mileage expiration policy less than a week later to protect miles for three years after any account activity, whether a member added to or sub- **Love may be eternal.** tracted from his or her **Miles and points are not.** account balance.

The following week, Delta embraced United's policy, which subsequently was adopted by most other major airlines, including American, and remains the de-facto industry standard today, except among the low cost carriers (see below).

Discounters Go Their Own Way

There are some significant exceptions to the three-year rule. Led by Southwest, whose successful business model has been emu- lated and revised by new generations of low cost carriers, some discount airlines have hobbled their programs with an expira- tion policy that traces its roots back to American's first effort:

Miles expire one year after they were earned and cannot be extended.

Southwest liberalized their one-year expiration policy in August 2005 to allow Rapid Rewards members two years to earn enough credits for an award. But the list of carriers that still have one-year rules includes AirTran, JetBlue and Independence Air.

Indianapolis based ATA also expires flight miles after 12 months, but allows miles earned from using its program-affiliated credit card to persist for 36 months. Even with Southwest now owning ATA, there are no plans to change these rules.

Deviating from other discounters, Denver based Frontier followed the lead of the full service airlines, including United, its principal competitor at Denver International Airport, in allowing miles to be extended by account activity, but uses a two-year extension period rather than the more widely used three years.

And just to prove there is no inherent reason why low cost carriers cannot be as generous in this area as full service airlines, America West operates its FlightFund program along the lines of mainline carrier programs, with a three-year rule on mileage expiration.

Combined with their limited partner rosters (JetBlue's program, for instance, has no airline or hotel partners) the one-year expiration schedule used by most discounters makes it difficult, or even impossible, for any but the most frequent flyers to earn a free trip in their programs.

Good Miles, Bad Miles

To some extent, changes over the past 24 years reflect the airlines' evolving relationships with frequent flyer miles; a relationship that is fundamentally ambivalent and likely will remain so.

For airlines and hotels, a mile or a point earned in their programs is both an investment and a liability.

On the one hand, a mile or a point earned in a company's loyalty program represents an investment by the consumer, giving that person a reason to continue doing business with that company, and with its program partners, in order to add more miles or points to his or her account and eventually reach an award threshold or to attain elite status. As marketers like to say, miles and points create "stickiness," another word for loyalty.

That is the marketing perspective on miles and points. It explains why, when American Airlines purchased many of bankrupt TWA's assets in 2001, American was willing to assume the liability represented by the billions of outstanding miles in the accounts of TWA Aviators members. By vesting TWA customers in American's program, American hoped to redirect their loyalty from TWA to American. In dollars and cents terms, the ticket sales generated by that loyalty were expected to more than cover the costs of free travel when miles were redeemed.

On the other hand, as executives on the airlines' financial sides will quickly point out, an earned mile represents an eventual cost to the loyalty program operator, but only if the member has enough miles in his or her account to qualify for an award. Because of this, a potential cost for flying an award passenger does exist. In accounting terms, this is called a contingent liability.

Bearing in mind the competing marketer and accountant perspectives, the commonplace assumption is that the airlines and hotels would like nothing better than to terminate your miles and points, sooner rather than later. This is not only simplistic but it is downright wrong.

Hotel Points

Major hotel programs are notably more conservative than their airline counterparts with regard to expiring program points. The rule in place at Best Western Gold Crown Club International, Hilton HHonors, Hyatt Gold Passport and Starwood Preferred Guest: points expire after 12 months if there is no account activity during that time.

In a slight departure from the norm, Marriott expires points in its Rewards program if no points are earned in a 24-month period.

Providing the exception to the rule that all things come to an end, Priority Club Rewards boasts that "points never expire" and that accounts remain in their system indefinitely, even when there is no activity.

For the significant number of hotel program participants electing to have their stays rewarded with airline miles rather than hotel points, the hotel programs' policies are a non-issue. But, for points earners in hotel programs with the one-year rule, vigilance is key to keeping accounts active.

Save the Miles

We have established that miles can expire and it goes without saying that losing miles is to be avoided if at all possible. So, how do you make sure your miles are not terminated?

First, all loyalty programs maintain policies regarding mileage expiration. Unfortunately, those policies are typically buried deep in the fine print of the programs' terms and conditions. Still, the policies are worth unearthing and then committing to memory. A mileage expiration schedule that does not square with your earning pace can put rewards out of reach, making program participation an exercise in futility and frustration.

It is important to monitor accounts, especially less active accounts, for impending expiration dates. If miles are about to expire, it only takes a single transaction to save them for another 36 months. That is particularly easy on the earning side, because the larger airline programs award miles for the purchase of just about any imaginable product or service through their extensive partner networks. (Do not forget the mileage malls that allow program members to earn miles for purchases at many popular online retailers.)

On the redemption side, short of using 25,000 miles for an award trip, there are fewer options. But, one low cost award now offered by most programs is magazine subscriptions, typically available for as few as 400 miles. Extend the life of your miles and get a year's subscription to *Popular Mechanics* or *Cosmopolitan*.

Other preventive measures include signing up for recurring services that earn miles. Phone or Internet services, for example, are billed monthly. So, using a company that awards frequent flyer miles for those kinds of services auto extends the life of your miles every month.

And of course another way of accomplishing the same thing is to use a loyalty program-affiliated credit card.

What to Do if Miles Expire

Expired miles are not always lost forever.

American recently launched a promotion, offering to reinstate AAdvantage members' expired miles for a fee ($50 for every 5,000 miles revived, plus a $30 processing fee). It is conceivable that this limited time opportunity will be written into AAdvantage as a permanent program feature. And from there, it would be a short step to mileage reinstatements becoming a standard offering among all large airline programs.

While consumers may welcome the flexibility of such a feature, the fees undermine its real world value. The cost to reactivate 25,000 miles, enough for a free domestic ticket in most programs, would be a hefty $280. For that price, you could purchase a revenue ticket on many routes without the bothersome capacity controls associated with restricted award tickets.

Although the American promotion is not the solution to the problem of expiring miles, it is a reminder that, as a practical matter, miles and points can be reinstated, provided the entire account was not deleted from the program's database. (An airline sometimes deletes inactive accounts simply so they are not taking up space on the airline's computers.) Since miles can be revived, it is worth throwing yourself onto the mercy of a customer service rep and requesting that your expired miles be reinstated. Ask for this favor in consideration of the business you have given the airline in the past and will promise to give them again in the future. Perhaps there was a compelling reason behind your lapse in loyalty. Or maybe there was a transaction that would have saved your miles but which, through no fault of your own, was never posted to your account.

Any number of approaches can be taken when petitioning to have miles returned to life. The important thing is not to take the expiration notice at face value. It never hurts to push back, gently, diplomatically and shrewdly.

Finally, the best approach is to keep miles from expiring in the first place. With the three-year rule and the multitude of earning options, there is no good reason to find yourself on the receiving end of the shattering news that, indeed, your miles have expired.

⊕ REMEMBER THIS:

> Know the mileage expiration policy of your programs.

> In the programs of the larger airlines, account activity every three years will extend the life of your miles indefinitely.

> Caveat: Miles in the programs of most discount carriers expire after just one or two years.

Chapter 16

The Best Frequent Flyer Advice You Will Ever Get

OK, WE DID PUT a lot of information in *Mileage Pro*. Information we hope you will be able to go back to time and time again. But we also know that your time is valuable and limited—especially if you are a road warrior and are out there traveling thousands of miles a year.

For easy reference, we have compiled the 52 best pieces of advice you will ever get regarding your frequent flyer miles. Please consider the following:

1. Eat out often. One of the fastest ways to a free trip is to skip airline food and go straight to your favorite restaurant. With several airlines now participating in mileage dining programs, a particular restaurant might offer from one to three to ten miles for every dollar you spend there. Still be careful. Some establishments require you to show your airline frequent flyer membership card, while others restrict visiting the same restaurant more than once a month to earn miles. Best advice: Join several airline dining programs such as the United Mileage Plus Dining or American AAdvantage Dining programs by Rewards Network. This is a great way for you to stay active in airline programs that have expiring miles. And you can use these miles to "top off" accounts in your less active programs. (Note: You can join more than one program, but you have to register different credit cards. The rule is that a given credit card can only be linked to one dining program at a time.)

2. *Be sociable.* Chat with airline seatmates as well as your coworkers to find out about new reward deals from other airlines and hotels. For instance, Marriott and Hilton members standing around the water cooler may hear about the "Faster Free Nights" program from Hyatt that awards one free night after two stays (without any point deduction) when paying by MasterCard.

3. *Carry a smaller wallet.* Gone are the days of excess. Pick one or two reward programs and put loyalty back into these programs. Leave your collection of membership cards (such as those only showing 732 total miles earned) at home.

4. *When there is no way to win the fight, relax.* With most major loyalty programs having miles that expire without activity over a three-year period, you must learn to manage the miles you earn. Staying active in your minor programs with some annual partner activity that will allow you to continue to save for a rainy day should be your strategy. Do not be fooled though. While miles may not expire, issued awards, such as free airline tickets, do. Normally, you have to use an award ticket within one year of it being issued.

5. Develop double vision. When one big reward program offers an unbeatable bonus opportunity, know that other programs will soon match. For example, in July 2005 when American introduced 750-mile distance awards for only 15,000 miles, United matched it just a few days later.

6. Do not be left standing inside the airport. Several programs allow you to exchange miles for airline club membership. Delta Platinum Medallion members get club membership for free allowing them, because of the SkyTeam alliance, to also visit the airline clubs of Continental and Northwest.

7. Avoid overlooking the obvious. Smaller and very substantial programs by Midwest Airlines and Frontier Airlines may be right under your nose. Now is the time to discover the difference.

8. Learn something new every week. For instance, did you know that some programs allow one-way awards at half the mileage requirements? Did you know that American AAdvantage has a formal program where they will match your elite membership on another airline when you meet certain flight requirements? For instance, if you are Premier Executive on United, American will match that status as long as you fly 15,000 miles on American in a three-month period. This is done to prove that you are capable of providing American a good amount of business. Listen and learn.

9. Double dip is not just for hotels. Multiply your miles on each trip by using only your airline program's car rental or hotel partners. Sticking with your airline's partners means you will not miss big opportunities. For example, on a flight from San Francisco to Denver you will earn 1,930 miles (roundtrip) depending on your airline program. The correct hotel partner could add an additional 500 bonus miles to that total, and a partner car rental could add another 50 to 250 bonus miles.

10. The real Double Dip. Opt for a hotel partner that lets you earn both miles (for the airline) and points (for the hotel). Hilton is the best example. Their Double Dip program now includes three options for you to customize each stay. You can choose HHonors Points and Variable Miles in which you earn 10 HHonors Base points plus one airline mile per eligible U.S. dollar spent. Or you can choose HHonors Points and Fixed Miles that earn 10 HHonors Base points per eligible U.S. dollar spent plus 500 airline bonus miles per stay (100 miles per stay at Hampton/Scandic hotels). Or you can choose HHonors Points with an extra bonus. By choosing just to earn HHonors points without airline miles, you will earn 10 HHonors Base points plus five bonus points per eligible U.S. dollar spent. Of the three choices, we often feel this option delivers the most value because it is the only option that will give you the choice to convert your points later on into miles as well as retain their value for use as hotel awards. The other two options convert everything automatically into miles leaving you without the ability to move them back into hotel points.

11. Know your programs. While you might be collecting miles, we always advise choosing points over miles with Marriott and Priority Club. The reason is simple: Both allow you to convert to miles at any time. If you choose miles right away, you will have forfeited your freedom of choice.

12. Building miles. You can build miles by buying a home. All major airline and hotel programs have national programs that will allow you to earn a lot of miles for mortgages. And guess what? Some of the nation's leading mortgage lenders (Countrywide, Washington Mutual Home Loans, Chase Home Finance, CitiMortgage and Wachovia Corporate Mortgage Services) participate in these programs.

13. Take advantage of special mileage earning promos. Hotels and car rental companies, along with airlines, offer bonus miles. Triple miles with an airline's car rental partners is a frequent promotion, while hotels often offer double and triple points by property. Become a real estate agent and find the hotel property that gives you the best bonus. These bonuses will be listed on the hotel program's Web site and in their member newsletter.

14. Be a mileage consumer while looking closely at your credit card choices. Flexibility is the name of the game and American Express and Diners Club are looking pretty good right now. P.S.: Did you know you could earn American, United and Northwest miles with the Starwood American Express card? (With the Starwood American Express card you earn Starwood points that can be converted into miles later on.) Did you know the Diners Club card is now accepted wherever MasterCard is accepted and also includes redemption with American, United and Northwest? We realize neither man nor woman will spend by one credit card alone. The best wallet has a Visa, a MasterCard and either an American Express or Diners Club card. The reason is need. Many hotel and other programs run promotions that earn extra bonus miles/points when paying with a particular type of credit card. So, do as the Boy Scouts do and always be prepared.

15. Be in the know. With an increasing number of incentive miles in the market, keep an eye out for free miles with the purchase of everything from dry cleaning services to automobiles. Did you know some residential utility companies, such as Gexa Energy in Texas, now offer miles for choosing them?

16. One of the hottest leads on learning more about any loyalty program is to surf the Internet. Newsy stuff and opinions, usually not found in print, can be found via Google or Yahoo!. Search term: frequent flyer (of course).

17. Capture all the points you can. For example, to make the most of choosing the best hotel program, be certain your hotel point total on your bill includes "total folio" rather than just earning points on the room rate. Who ever thought "room service" could be so tasty?

18. Study hard. It is now fashionable to actually read your loyalty program's newsletter. Most have changed to electronic delivery and many are now rich with special bonus offers that can up your mileage or hotel point balance. Note: These newsletters are the only place you will find out about the latest auction of miles that may send you to the Super Bowl for free. And most programs give you miles or points for signing up to receive their newsletters.

19. Withdraw miles. Need miles for an award this year? If so, move the exact number of miles from your Priority Club, American Express Membership Rewards, Diners Club Rewards or Starwood programs into your primary airline program. Never, ever turn more points into miles than you actually need. While you will not lose the miles or points, they just will not be where you want them. More of a hassle factor.

20. Take a second look. OK, you are a hotel kind of person who stays at Brand X. But, if you have not looked lately, Choice Hotels may be the sleeper program of the year. Many new rewards (no blackout dates) and positive changes in their program. Our advice: Take a second look at programs you normally do not do a lot of business with.

21. Play your points. Got points and need miles? Hold on and play the odds. Did you know that for the past five years Diners Club has offered a bonus redemption of 50 percent or greater when converting their points into British Airways Executive Club miles? Or that American Express Membership Rewards annually offers a bonus of 15 to 30 percent when redeeming into Continental or Delta miles?

22. Use points or miles to underwrite a vacation. If you are a light traveler (you have not racked up anything close to what you need for a significant award in an airline or hotel program) but are a heavy duty shopper, you can earn miles and points when shopping online at merchants such as The Gap, Tommy Hilfiger, Barnes & Noble, Best Buy, Body Shop and our favorite, Mrs. Field's Cookies. Nearly every major loyalty program has a portal for earning miles or points while shopping online. We will see you at the "virtual" checkout line.

23. Designate a primary airline. You probably belong to three or four airline programs. If you fly on one airline 75 percent of the time, or more than 10,000 miles on one carrier in a year, then make that your major program.

24. Do the whole deal. Hotel programs often offer vacation packages you can purchase with points. Believe it or not, it is now possible to earn a free hotel, airline ticket and car rental with one reward. Talk about convenient.

25. *Qualify for elite membership.* Nothing is as important as earning elite status in your primary loyalty programs. Verify the number of miles needed to qualify in both your airline and hotel programs. It is well worth scheduling an extra flight or night in a hotel if that is all that stands between you and the extensive benefits of elite membership.

26. *Buy online.* Most programs offer you the opportunity to earn bonus miles if you purchase tickets directly from the airline's Web site. Beam up those miles from United, American, Alaska and US Airways.

27. *Loyalty is not dead.* Know your major program's partners (airline, hotel, car rental) and stick with them.

28. *Rack up free nights.* Once you have earned enough miles for free air travel, start opting for points instead of miles in your hotel program. By booking enough stays you can get free lodging to use with your flight award for an almost free vacation (since you still have to pay for meals and other incidentals).

29. *Phone home?* Although there are not as many telephone partners as in years past, owing to the popularity of cell phone use, that does not mean these programs do not exist. Quiz your frequent flyer friends to find out who is still earning bonus miles for talking on the phone. We would tell you here but that is not possible because the partners and offers change too frequently. Sorry.

30. *Educate yourself.* Read the fine print instead of just the headlines and become a true mileage expert. Know when you can and cannot earn miles for elite qualification. For example, mileage earned on some special promotional flights, some code shares and even some partner flights may not accrue toward elite status. Conversely, some credit card purchases now qualify toward elite status credit.

31. Learn how to stretch your miles. If your three-year stash is about to expire, tap a small partner such as a car rental company or a dining program to keep those miles active. No need to fly or stay at a hotel. Just use your knowledge of how to stay "active" for another three years.

32. Listen to the music. Buy your iPod music and earn points for each dollar spent on music downloads. Points can be earned for Priority Club Rewards and Marriott Rewards. Tip: No airline currently offers this option but you could convert these hotel points into airline miles.

33. Plan ahead. Many programs have raised the cost of certain fees associated with express service for an award. Plan ahead and your award will remain free.

34. Gotta have it. Capacity controls got you down? With all the miles you earn from these tips you might need to use some to get the exact reward seat you want. Capacity free awards are available from all major airline programs and from most hotel programs but they do cost more miles.

35. Privileges. Do not forget that in some hotel programs, elite and other members qualify for free breakfast credit. Eat for free!

36. Respect others. Several loyalty programs administer employee recognition programs to reward those who provide great service. Do yourself and them a favor by participating. When a recognition program is offered, you will receive a recognition card to present to the employee who then submits it for reward credit. Sometimes you will even get small ribbons to hand out to deserving airline or hotel employees.

37. Do not forget to back up. This advice is not about computers. It is a reminder to always carry your complete list of frequent traveler program numbers around with you in case you are ever bumped from a flight and end up flying on another carrier. You will have the right frequent flyer number at hand and will not have to send in for missing credit. The trick? Make a complete list of all your program numbers on a small sheet of paper, have it laminated, and carry it in your wallet.

38. Tick tock. In November, do not become the turkey by letting your miles expire. Now is the time to find out if any of your miles or points will depart this Earth at year's end.

39. Be a savvy mileage spender. Some programs offer you the chance to redeem awards for fewer miles. American AAdvantage has special awards for Citibank credit card holders, and both American and United give special discounted awards when you fly 750 miles or less.

40. Cash in by converting. One trend you need to know about is that more programs now allow you to convert airline miles for more than just free flights. Frontier Airlines has the More Store that allows members to cash in for dining certificates, a new car and even bicycles. Both American and United now have miles for hotel rooms. Beyond that even more airlines are expected to come up with even more fresh ideas and offers.

41. Pool your efforts. For instance, for a fee the American AAdvantage program will allow members to move miles from one member's account into another member's account. These "pooled" miles often go to friends or family as gifts. These "pooling options" require a transfer fee but for the right situation it may just be the key to a free ticket for someone else in your family. Most major airline programs now have this option either as a benefit for members or as a promotional offer several times a year.

42. Shoot for a million miles in a single program. More airlines than ever before are putting together programs that honor those who fly them the most. What is cool about earning a million miles, other than having the right to brag, is that an airline with a million miles program also gives you lifetime elite privileges.

43. Spread your mileage around. With a large balance in your primary program, you can afford a more diversified portfolio of miles and points in several secondary programs. This allows you to grab even more awards and helps you bypass any sold-out award situations.

44. Top off accounts. Membership in several programs means you need to diversify your earnings to maintain the balances required for the awards you have targeted. Consider adding miles earned by dining, credit card, telephone and other third-party partners. And do not forget the sign-up bonuses.

45. Stay alert. Many international travelers must contend with changing itineraries. Keep an eye out for new airline partners in the various global alliances.

46. Suck up every bonus you can on international travel. Travelers who hit world capitals on a regular basis are prime candidates for bonuses. One trip to Asia in the right cabin class could earn you one free domestic ticket, as long as you register to earn the bonus (registration is usually required). For example, in October 2005, British Airways launched a bonus for travel across the Atlantic in which members who registered could earn a guaranteed 50,000 frequent flyer miles for a single trip. It was a combination of the miles earned from flying along with bonus miles. Referred to as a "long haul" bonus, it is worth more than almost all the bonuses you might earn by traveling solely within the United States.

47. Protect ALL your miles. Having substantial earnings in one or several programs means you have more to lose if you lose track. Note the expiration dates of any miles and awards you have earned. Better yet, start thinking about using awards today that you might normally put off using until tomorrow. Some members rely on managing their miles with their memories, while others use homemade spreadsheets, or even worse not managing their miles at all. We feel strongly that an investment in one of the program management software solutions (see Resources for the Mileage Junkies on page 183) can protect all your miles with no additional investment of your time.

48. Minimize mileage expiration. Many mega milers find they do not have enough time to use all their awards and miles. If you find yourself up against deadlines, familiarize yourself with the Hilton HHonors Reward Exchange and Points.com. These nifty exchange options allow you to trade your unexpired miles from one program to another. There are restrictions as to which programs participate, but at least your miles will not expire. But frankly, with the dilution of miles or points, you might be better off keeping them. Dilution occurs when you move miles or points from one program, through a middleman, such as Points.com, and then to miles or points within another program. Often members will lose 50 to 90 percent of the miles' or points' original values. If you are wondering why this is, it is because loyalty programs were introduced to try to make you loyal to a single program. If you want choices, it is going to cost you.

49. Do not lose sight of any opportunity. When your mileage balance reaches a high level, you may think you have perfected the art of accrual or you may think some promotional offers do not merit your attention. Not so in either case. Keep reading newsletters. Periodically review all the ways you can capture miles to make sure you have covered all the bases.

50. Splurge. How about attending the British Open, the Super Bowl or any number of unique events? With a wealth of auction packages from which to choose, consider bidding on the special events and unusual vacations offered by airlines and hotel programs. In the past, United Mileage Plus has even allowed members to bid their miles for a part in a TV sitcom. Auctions vary by loyalty program. Some auctions are open to all members, such as the auction in the Continental OnePass program. In the past, other programs such as American AAdvantage only had auctions for elite members, which is something even smaller programs like Frontier Airlines EarlyReturns are doing. Auctions are not only conducted by the airlines. Hilton HHonors sponsored recent auctions allowing members to attend the Academy Awards, and in a variation, American

Express recently gave members the opportunity to redeem their points (as little as 5,000 of them) for a Mercedes Benz.

51. Donate miles. Have miles you cannot use? Give them to a charity. Virtually every airline and hotel program can funnel miles and points to a variety of organizations such as Americares, CARE, Make a Wish, National Children's Cancer Society and the United Way. And we can answer a question before you even ask it: We are sorry but the IRS has determined that donating your miles to a worthy and charitable cause is not tax deductible.

52. Registered traveler. Do not confuse this with the government airport security program. Almost every traveler we know has missed out on collecting bonus miles because they failed to register for a promotion. These days, loyalty programs require you to register for a bonus rather than automatically issuing you the extra miles and points. Make sure you know when registering is a requirement. For instance, members of the Delta SkyMiles credit card by American Express could have earned double miles for every purchase they made over a two-month period if they had registered their card number. Those who did not were only able to earn a single mile per every dollar spent.

Chapter 17

Resources for Mileage Junkies

Frequent Travel Programs

The final authority on program terms and conditions, promotions and partnerships are the airlines, hotels, car rental companies and credit card companies hosting each program.

KEY

Telephone: A point of contact

URL: Web site address

Expiration: These are the rules regarding the expiration of the program's miles, points and credits.

Account Pooling: These are the rules regarding transferring miles, points or credits from one member's account into another member's account. This is not information for redeeming awards for other individuals.

Transferable: If applicable, we note the program's rules on transferring miles. Unless noted, the program default is award transferability to anyone.

Alliance Member: If applicable, the alliance the airline is affiliated with is listed.

Airline Programs

AeroMexico

Club Premier

Telephone: 1-800-247-3737

URL: www.aeromexico.com

Expiration: Kilometers accrued in the Club Premier account never expire; you just have to fly on an AM code flight at the full public fare price once every 24 months.

Account Pooling: Club Premier benefits may be assigned to anyone designated by the member at the moment of requesting them. In the case of requesting a Club Premier award ticket for an international flight, the name of the beneficiary must match the name on his or her passport.

Alliance Member: Club Premier is a member of the SkyTeam alliance.

Air Canada

Aeroplan

Telephone: 1-800-361-5373

URL: www.aeroplan.com

Expiration: After three years without any transactions the account can be deleted. New members have 12 months to earn miles before the account is closed.

Account Pooling: On occasion, members can participate in promotions to transfer miles among member accounts at two cents (CND) per miles transferred with a minimum of 1,000 miles.

Alliance Member: Aeroplan is a member of the Star Alliance.

AirTran

A+ Rewards

Telephone: 1-800-AIR-TRAN; 1-888-3-APLUS-8

URL: www.aplusrewards.com

Expiration: One year

Transferable: Elite members may only transfer miles to other members' accounts.

Alliance Member: A+ Rewards is not a member of any alliance.

Alaska Airlines

Mileage Plan

Telephone: 1-800-622-2680

URL: www.alaskaair.com

Expiration: Three years from transaction

Account Pooling: No

Alliance Member: Mileage Plan is not a member of any alliance.

Aloha Airlines

AlohaPass

Telephone: 1-800-252-5642

URL: www.alohaairlines.com

Expiration: None.

Account Pooling: No

Alliance Member: AlohaPass is not a member of any alliance.

America West

FlightFund

Telephone: 1-800-247-5691

URL: www.flightfund.com

Expiration: 36 months from transaction

Account Pooling: No

Alliance Member: FlightFund is not a member of any alliance.

Remarks: This program is scheduled to merge with US Airways Dividend Miles. Details were not available when *Mileage Pro* was printed.

American Airlines

AAdvantage

Telephone: 1-800-421-0600

URL: www.aa.com

Expiration: 36 months from transaction

Account Pooling: Yes, a maximum of 60,000 miles per year can be transferred. You need to pay a transaction fee.

Alliance Member: AAdvantage is a member of the oneworld alliance.

ATA

Travel Awards

Telephone: 1-800-I-FLY-ATA

URL: www.ata.com

Expiration: 12 months. Points earned through your ATA Visa will expire three years from the date they are posted to your ATA Travel Awards account.

Account Pooling: No

Alliance Member: Travel Awards is not a member of any alliance.

British Airways

Executive Club

Telephone: 1-800-955-2748

URL: www.britishairways.com

Expiration: After three years without transaction the account can be deleted.

Account Pooling: Yes. The Household Account enables you to pool with up to six other members of your household.

Alliance Member: British Airways is a member of the oneworld alliance.

Continental Airlines

OnePass

Telephone: 1-713-952-1630

URL: www.onepass.com

Expiration: After 18 months Continental can delete the account.

Account Pooling: No

Alliance Member: OnePass is a member of the SkyTeam alliance.

Delta Air Lines

SkyMiles

Telephone: 1-800-323-2323

URL: www.delta.com

Expiration: 36 months from transaction

Account Pooling: No

Alliance Member: SkyMiles is a member of the SkyTeam alliance.

Frontier Airlines

EarlyReturns

Telephone: 1-866-263-2759

URL: www.flyfrontier.com

Expiration: Two years

Account Pooling: No

Alliance Member: EarlyReturns is not a member of any alliance.

Hawaiian Airlines

HawaiianMiles

Telephone: 1-877-HA-MILES

URL: www.hawaiianair.com

Expiration: Three years

Account Pooling: Miles can be transferred up to 10 times a year.

Alliance Member: HawaiianMiles is not a member of any alliance.

Independence Air

iCLUB

Telephone: 1-800-FLY-FLYi

URL: www.flyi.com

Expiration: 12 months

Account Pooling: No

Alliance Member: iCLUB is not a member of any alliance.

Japan Airlines

JAL Mileage Bank

Telephone: 1-800-JAL-MILE

URL: www.japanair.com

Expiration: At the end of the calendar year of the third year after account activity.

Account Pooling: No, but members who are registered under the same JAL Family Club (JFC) membership will be able to combine accrued mileage only at the time of redeeming mileage for JMB awards as one of the JFC membership benefits.

Alliance Member: Mileage Bank is not a member of any alliance.

Lufthansa

Miles & More

Telephone: 1-800-581-6400

URL: www.milesandmore.com

Expiration: 36 months from transaction

Account Pooling: No

Alliance Member: Miles & More is a member of the Star Alliance.

Mexicana

Frecuenta

Telephone: 1-800-531-7901

URL: www.mexicana.com

Expiration: The earned miles do not expire. Nevertheless, the member's account will be purged within three years if the account does not indicate activity.

Account Pooling: If the cardholder of the account dies, the earned miles in his account cannot be transferred to anyone else, for which reason both the account as well as the miles will be cancelled. Therefore, the miles cannot be inherited in the case of the death of the member. Frecuenta mileage credit is not transferable and may not be combined or transferred among or to Frecuenta members, members' estates, successors and assigns. Miles cannot be transferred between Frecuenta members and/or corporations (enterprises).

Alliance Member: Frecuenta left the Star Alliance in 2004.

Midwest Airlines

Midwest Miles

Telephone: 1-800-314-7125

URL: www.midwestmiles.com

Expiration: Miles expire after 36 months with no earning activity. Accounts without earning activity in the first 12 months after enrollment may be deleted.

Account Pooling: No

Alliance Member: Midwest Miles is not a member of any alliance.

Northwest Airlines

WorldPerks

Telephone: 1-800-447-3757

URL: www.nwa.com

Expiration: Three years from account earning activity

Account Pooling: Yes. You can transfer up to 50,000 miles per year to other WorldPerks members. You need to pay a transfer fee.

Alliance Member: WorldPerks is a member of the SkyTeam alliance.

Southwest Airlines

Rapid Rewards

Telephone: 1-800-445-5764;
1-800-I-FLY-SWA

URL: www.rapidrewards.com

Expiration: Each credit is valid for
24 months from the date earned.

Account Pooling: No

Alliance Member: Rapid Rewards
is not a member of any alliance.

United Airlines

Mileage Plus

Telephone: 1-800-421-4655

URL: www.mileageplus.com

Expiration: 36 months from transaction; 12 months after enrollment

Account Pooling: No, but there
are time-limited promotions
where you can transfer miles
to other accounts.

Alliance Member: Mileage Plus
is a member of the Star Alliance.

US Airways

Dividend Miles

Telephone: 1-336-661-8390

URL: www.usairways.com

Expiration: 36 months from
transaction.

Account Pooling: No

Alliance Member: Dividend Miles
is a member of the Star Alliance.

Virgin Atlantic Airways

flying club

Telephone: 1-800-821-5438

URL: www.virgin-atlantic.com

Expiration: Both your miles and
membership will remain active
provided you complete a Virgin
Atlantic or partner earning or
spending activity in any three-year
period.

Account Pooling: Miles earned
through a family account will be
transferred automatically into the
Gold member's account after each
mileage transaction is complete.

Alliance Member: Flying Club
is not a member of any alliance.

Hotel Programs

Best Western

Gold Crown Club

Telephone: 1-800-237-8483

URL: www.goldcrownclub.com

Expiration: To prevent your points
or membership from expiring,
simply stay at a Best Western
at a qualified rate at least once
during a 12-month period.

Account Pooling: Points can be
pooled if both members share
the same address.

Choice Hotels

Choice Privileges

Telephone: 1-800-521-2121

URL: www.choiceprivileges.com

Expiration: Choice Privileges Points
expire on December 31, two years
after the year in which they were
deposited into your account unless
forfeited or canceled earlier due to
membership inactivity or otherwise in accordance to these rules
and regulations.

Account Pooling: You may not transfer your points to anyone or by any means, including through a will or through a divorce decree.

Hilton Hotels

HHonors

Telephone: 1-800-HHONORS

URL: www.hiltonhhonors.com

Expiration: Members who do not earn points in any 12 consecutive month period may be removed from the program.

Account Pooling: HHonors points and airline miles are not transferable but awards may be issued to other persons.

Hyatt Hotels

Gold Passport

Telephone: 1-800-228-3360

URL: www.goldpassport.com

Expiration: The Hyatt Gold Passport program may continue until such time as Hyatt Gold Passport, at its sole discretion, elects to designate a program termination date. Hyatt Gold Passport has the right to end the Hyatt Gold Passport program by providing written notice to then Active Members six months in advance. An "Active Member" is a member who has received Hyatt Gold Passport points or Airline miles within the preceding 12 months. A member's Hyatt Gold Passport membership may be discontinued at Hyatt Gold Passport's discretion if a member does not record Hyatt Gold Passport points or airline miles

activity during any consecutive 12-month period. All Hyatt Gold Passport points in the account will be forfeited at that time.

Account Pooling: Hyatt Gold Passport points are for member's benefit only and are not transferable to another person for any reason including divorce or inheritance. In the case of documented death of a Hyatt Gold Passport member, Hyatt Gold Passport points are transferable to a person sharing the same residential mailing address. Hyatt Gold Passport members may request that a Hyatt Gold Passport award be issued to another individual.

Jameson Inn/Signature Inn

Stock Awards

Telephone: 1-800-526-3766

URL: www.jamesoninn.com

Expiration: Earned shares of stock do not expire

Account Pooling: No

InterContinental Hotels Group

Priority Club Rewards

Telephone: 1-888-211-9874

URL: www.priorityclub.com

Expiration: An active member is defined as any member having point activity (accrual or redemption) within the last 12 months.

Account Pooling: Priority Club Rewards points may be transferred between any two specifically designated member accounts. A member may authorize the transfer of the necessary number of Priority Club Rewards points into another member's account. The cost to the member authorizing the transfer will be $5 USD per 1,000 points transferred, and can only be paid for by an accepted credit card. Follow the instructions at www.priorityclub.com/transferpoints or call your regional Priority Club®Service Center for assistance. An Authorization to Transfer Points form must be completed and submitted in order to transfer the required number of points. Once the authorization for transfer is received and processed, the transferor relinquishes all rights to the transferred points. No cancellations or refunds are permitted. Other than as stated above, no transfer of points may occur.

La Quinta Hotels

Returns

Telephone: 1-800-642-4258

URL: www.yourreturns.com

Expiration: Points earned will be issued as of the date of check-in and will expire 24 months from the check-in date. Members who do not have any stay activity within a 12-month consecutive period will be removed from the program and all accrued points will be forfeited.

Account Pooling: Returns points have no fixed value, may not be redeemed for cash and are not transferable. The transfer of reward certificates or other Returns benefits for value (whether by sale or exchange of goods or services) by a member is prohibited. Any points, certificates or benefits that

La Quinta deems to have been sold, transferred, or assigned in violation of these terms and conditions may be canceled or confiscated.

Loews Hotels

Loews First

Telephone: 1-800-LOEWS12

URL: www.loews-first.com

Expiration: You will be considered an "Active Member" as long as you have stayed in a Loews Hotel during the previous 12 months.

Account Pooling: Membership benefits apply for the member only and are not transferable.

Marriott Hotels

Marriott Rewards

Telephone: 1-800-450-4442 (automated); 1-801-468-4000

URL: www.marriottrewards.com

Expiration: An account may be closed at Marriott's discretion if no points are accrued during a 24-month period. All points in the account will be forfeited at that time.

Account Pooling: Points accrued by a Marriott Rewards member are for the member's benefit only and may not be transferred to anyone. Points are transferable to a legal spouse only in the case of documented death of the member. Points are not transferable to another person for any other reason, including divorce or inheritance.

Omni Hotels

Select Guest

Telephone: 1-877-440-OMNI

URL: www.selectguest.com

Expiration: N/A

Account Pooling: N/A

Radisson Hotels

goldpoints plus

Telephone: 1-888-288-8889

URL: www.goldpointsplus.com

Expiration: Do not expire

Account Pooling: Gold Points can be transferred from one card account to another if (1) both cards have been enrolled, and (2) if the transfer is between program members in the same household (having the same principal residence), and (3) if a written authorization to transfer Gold Points is signed by both parties and sent to the goldpoints plus contact center.

Red Lion/WestCoast Hotels

Guest Awards

Telephone: 1-800-325-4000

URL: www.guestawards.com

Expiration: A member's Guest Awards points will expire if there is not any Red Lion or WestCoast Hotel stay activity that occurs during any calendar year. Expired points cannot be reinstated.

Account Pooling: Guest Awards points may not be pooled with or transferred to other awards programs or accounts. Guest Awards offers program membership to individual accounts only and not

to corporations or other entities. You may establish and maintain only one member account.

Starwood Hotels

Starwood Preferred Guest

Telephone: 1-888-625-4988

URL: www.spg.com

Expiration: You will be considered an "Active Member" so long as you have earned Starpoints as a result of activities at participating Starwood Properties or as a result of use of the Starwood Preferred Guest Credit Card from American Express during the previous 12 months.

Account Pooling: Starpoints may be transferred between two specifically designated Preferred Guest accounts sharing the same residential mailing address with the exception of Starwood Vacation Ownership Preferred Guest account. Starwood Vacation Ownership Owners may transfer Starpoints between two designated Starwood Vacation Ownership and Starwood Preferred Guest accounts, regardless of whether or not the residential mailing address is the same on both accounts.

Cendant Hotels

TripRewards

Telephone: 1-800-367-8747

URL: www.triprewards.com

Expiration: TripRewards points expire four years after being posted to the member's account, unless forfeited or cancelled earlier due to membership inactivity.

Account Pooling: TripRewards points in a member's account do not constitute property of the member, have no cash value, and cannot be transferred during or after the member's life, by operation of law or otherwise.

Rental Car Programs

Avis

Preferred Select Rewards

Telephone: 1-800-230-4898

URL: www.avis.com

Expiration: To qualify for rewards, rentals must be completed during an 18-month period.

Account Pooling: No

Remarks: For U.S. residents only

Hertz

Hertz #1 Club

Telephone: 1-800-654-3131

URL: www.hertz.com

Expiration: None

Account Pooling: No

Remarks: Participation in the #1 Awards program is limited to residents of the United States, U.S.V.I., Puerto Rico, and certain U.S. territories. Minimum age for enrollment in Hertz #1 Club is 25 (exceptions apply).

National

Emerald Club

Telephone: 1-800-962-7070

URL: www.emeraldclub.com

Expiration: Each member's credits will remain valid as long as such member is a member of the program. Each Emerald Club member remains active as long as he or she completes at least one vehicle rental with National Car Rental in each calendar year.

Account Pooling: No

Thrifty

Blue Chip

Telephone: 1-888-400-8877

URL: www.thrifty.com/bluechip

Expiration: Earned reward certificates are valid for one year from date of issue.

Account Pooling: No

Credit Card Programs

American Express

Membership Rewards

Telephone: 1-800-AXP-EARN

URL: www.membershiprewards.com

Expiration: Points have no expiration date as long as you maintain a Membership Rewards account with an eligible, enrolled card.

Account Pooling: Several cards can be connected to a single Membership Rewards account.

Diners Club

Club Rewards

Telephone: 1-800-234-4034

URL: www.dinersclubus.com

Expiration: There is no limit to the number of points you can earn, and your points do not expire as long as your account is open and current.

Account Pooling: Club Rewards points cannot be transferred to any other Club Rewards [or other charge card] account at any time.

Miscellaneous Programs

Amtrak

Guest Rewards

Telephone: 1-800-307-5000

URL: www.amtrakguestrewards.com

Expiration: Points earned under the program will not expire as long as the program continues and the member purchases travel on Amtrak within a three-year period and provides sufficient documentation of such travel to Amtrak within at least 30 days of the member's travel. Amtrak Guest Rewards points expire three years after your last Amtrak travel purchase.

Account Pooling: Points cannot be combined with cash or another member's points to obtain a reward.

Independent Information and Advice

Following are a number of independent Web sites and newsletters that provide frequent-flyer program related information, commentary and advice. (As indicated, the authors of this book publish, edit or contribute to a number of the listed publications.)

AwardPlanner.com: Web site for assisting members of frequent flyer programs, specializing in redeeming miles and points for members of these programs. If you do not have the time it takes to plan your next award travel or are having difficulty getting the awards you want, then this site just may be your ticket. [1]

MileDonor.com: A comprehensive collection of news, links and information to help members of all frequent flyer programs donate their miles, points and credits to charities and other worthy causes. [1]

FlyerTalk.com: With nearly five million posts by members, this Web site is dedicated to members of frequent flyer programs worldwide. Travelers who log on help each other with advice on earning and burning their favorite loyalty currency. [1]

FlyerTalkWiki.com: The world's first collaborative project listing frequent flyer programs from around the world with their rules, award charts, partners, elite levels and program basics.

FreeFrequentFlyerMiles.com: A handy resource for members of frequent flyer programs seeking information on how to earn frequent flyer miles without flying. Contains many links to various partner offers.

FrequentFlier.com: One of two Web sites exclusively developed for frequent flyer program information and advice. Includes member bulletin board. [2]

FrequentFlier Crier: The weekly news and information newsletter for the frequentflier.com Web site. [2]

FrequentFlyerBonuses.com: Another handy resource for members of frequent flyer programs seeking information on how to earn frequent flyer miles without flying. Contains many links to a variety of partner offers.

FrequentFlyer.oag.com: Updated twice monthly, this Web site covers news and information about a variety of frequent flyer programs, including reward deals and promotions, and topical features such as expiring miles, award redemption and more. Information is also included in the magazine's e-newsletter, *OAG Frequent Flyer Update.* [3] [4]

InsideFlyer: Published since 1986, *InsideFlyer* is the only print publication in the world delivering news, information and advice to members of frequent flyer programs. Published monthly. [1]

MaxMiles.com: Another Web site devoted to helping members of frequent flyer programs list all their programs in a single statement designed to help members manage their miles and points.

MileAlert: The bi-weekly news and information e-newsletter for the SmarterTravel.com Web site. [3]

MileMarker (webflyer.com): A clever tool showing you distances between city and trip pairs, MileMarker was designed to let you know the number of miles earned with each flight. Options include elite and other bonuses. Handy for determining the number of flights needed at year's end to re-qualify for elite status. [1]

Mileage Converter (webflyer.com): Tool allowing members of various frequent flyer programs to determine how they can convert miles or points from one program to another. Includes redemption rates and instructions. [1]

Mileage Mall (webflyer.com): Handy tool that highlights and links to various online shopping offers to earn additional frequent flyer miles. Options include shopping by mall, store or bonus offer. [1]

MileageManager (www.mileagemanager.com: Most members of frequent flyer programs do not "manage" their miles and points very well. This tool is devoted exclusively to that purpose and features "alerts" designed to help members avoid expiring miles, to be aware of all current bonus offers, and to have access to award charts. [1]

MilesLink: The bi-weekly news and information e-newsletter for the webflyer.com Web site. [1]

PayAnythingOnline.com: A clever Web site designed to help members with frequent flyer credit cards pay any bill to earn additional frequent flyer miles. Handy for rent or mortgage payments or any other bills that do not accept credit cards. There is a transaction fee of 2.89 percent, which may or may not make the activity worthwhile.

PointsWizard.com: Changing business model now makes this Web site a listing of news articles regarding frequent flyer programs.

Rewards Canada (www.rewardscanada.ca): See frequentflyerbonuses.com.

OAG.com: This Web site lists airport information, destination guides and other travel related information. Travelers can also pay to view worldwide flight schedules. [5]

SmarterTravel.com: While not devoted exclusively to the topic of frequent flyer information, this Web site has a respectable amount of news articles and information helpful to members of these programs. [3]

ViewFromTheWing (www.blogs.flyertalk.com): A frequent flyer programs blog, updated daily with news and information from the mouth of an avid frequent flyer Gary Leff. Entertaining and worthy of a daily read. [1]

WebFlyer.com: One of two Web sites exclusively developed for frequent flyer program information and advice. [1]

[1] Part of the WebFlyer network headed by Randy Petersen, a co-author of this book.
[2] Written and published by Tim Winship, a co-author of this book.
[3] Tim Winship is a contributing editor for these publications.
[4] Published by *Frequent Flyer* magazine, which is owned by the publisher of this book, OAG Worldwide Inc.
[5] Owned by the publisher of this book, OAG Worldwide Inc.

General Travel Resources

Finally, we list some favorite sources for travel information.

Airline Codes: www.avrefdesk.com/two_letter_airline_codes.htm. A list of the world's airlines and their two-letter codes.

Air Travel: www.faa.gov/passengers. The Federal Aviation Administration's official site includes airline safety and performance data and it also logs airline-related complaints.

Airline Reservations Numbers: www.airlinenumbers.com. A simple list of U.S. and international airlines' reservations numbers.

Airline Seating: www.seatguru.com. Seating charts for many airlines, including legroom, seat pitch, exit rows, and proximity to the bathrooms.

Airport Codes: www.world-airport-codes.com. Comprehensive searchable database of the three-letter airport and city codes.

Airport Maps: www.mapquest.com/maps/airport.adp. A little-known feature of MapQuest.com is that this site features maps of many U.S. airports.

Airport Status: www.fly.faa.gov/flyfaa/usmap.jsp. The FAA's guide to airport (versus flight-specific) delays.

ATM Locators:
www.visa.com/atms and
www.mastercard.com/atmlocator.
Find an ATM just about anywhere.

Currency Converters:
www.xe.com/ucc. Also,
www.oanda.com has a nifty
take-it-with-you currency cheat
sheet (follow the "Travel" link).

Customs:
www.cbp.gov/xp/cgov/travel. The
official Bureau of U.S. Customs and
Border Protection site publishes a
"Know Before You Go" fact sheet
with details about items that can
and can't be taken into the country,
and the rules regarding duty fees.

Discount Airlines:
www.whichbudget.com. A list of
low-fare airlines by destination or
originating city.

Flight Status: www.flightview.com.
Track flights by flight number,
airline, departure time.

Health: www.cdc.gov/travel. The
Web site of the Centers for Disease
Control and Prevention includes
health-related travel information
and tips.

Hotel Reservations Numbers:
www.hotelnumbers.com. List of
hotel chains' reservations numbers.

International Dialing Codes:
www.countrycallingcodes.com.
Displays dial codes for calling
between many countries.

Maps: www.mapquest.com. The
leading site for U.S. maps and
directions. For European maps,
try www.viamichelin.com.

Security: www.tsa.gov. The Web
page for the Transportation
Security Administration (TSA),
including historical security line
clearance times at most U.S.
airports and security tips. The
U.S. Department of State Web
site (www.travel.state.gov)
includes travel warnings for
countries deemed dangerous
for foreign visitors and other
overseas travel advice.

Travel Documents:
www.travel.state.gov/passport/
index.html. Information from the
State Department on obtaining
new and replacement passports.
Applications and other forms can
be downloaded from the site.

Travel Insurance:
www.insuremytrip.com,
www.quotetravelinsurance.com.
Sites compare packages and
prices from multiple insurers.

World Time:
www.timeanddate.com/worldclock.
Current time and date in many
cities worldwide.

Weather: www.weather.com.
Displays current weather by
zip code or city.

Wi-Fi Access Points:
www.jiwire.com. Searchable list
of Wi-Fi hotspots, both free and
fee-based.

Chapter 18
Glossary of Key Mileage Related Terms

*A: The acronym stands for the Star Alliance, which features United, Lufthansa, Air Canada and Singapore Airlines as members.

1K: United Mileage Plus Premier Executive 1K status. Awarded to members who fly 100,000 actual miles or 100 paid segments in a single calendar year.

1P: United Mileage Plus Premier Executive status. Awarded to members who fly 50,000 miles or 60 segments in a single calendar year.

2P: United Mileage Plus Premier status. Awarded to members who fly 25,000 actual miles or 30 paid segments in a single calendar year.

ACCRUAL: The accumulation of frequent traveler program miles and points through actual travel, partner bonuses and special promotions.

ACTUAL MILES: The physical distance that a flight covers. When calculating actual miles, class of service, elite level status and other bonuses are not included.

ADVANCE PURCHASE: A condition imposed on "Restricted Tickets," which means tickets must be bought seven, 14 or 21 days before the departure date of the first flight.

AFFINITY CARD: Credit or charge cards in partnership with a particular airline or hotel frequent travel program. Charges to the card earn miles or points, which either accrue directly into the associated program or can be transferred into it.

ALLIANCE: A group of airlines allowing frequent flyer program members to earn miles or points and enjoy special benefits when flying with any participating airline. The miles or points can, in turn, be used for an award ticket on any alliance airlines.

APEX: Industry jargon for "Advance Purchase," from "advance-purchase excursion fare."

AUCTION: An award sale through which program members use their miles to bid against each other for a one-time only award that often involves attending special events or meeting famous people.

AWARD: Free airline ticket, hotel stay or night, rental car, merchandise item, traveler's check or gift certificate. Depending on the program, awards may mean actual tickets or just certificates that need to be redeemed at airline ticket counters, hotel front desks, car rental desks or specific merchandise outlets. This term is interchangeable with "reward."

BASE MILES: Typically used to denote "Flight Miles," and exclude class-of-service bonuses, promotional bonuses and elite qualifying miles.

BETWEEN (versus TO/FROM): In determining routing for accrual travel or award travel, "between" indicates that travel may originate on either end of a route. For example, a roundtrip award that allows travel between Mexico and the United States means that travel can originate in either Mexico or the United States. Conversely, roundtrip travel to Mexico from the United States means that travel is restricted and must originate and terminate in the United States.

BLACKOUT DATES: Certain days during high-traffic seasons when airline and hotel award travel is restricted or not available. Note: This term is often confused with "Capacity Controls."

BOARDING PASS: Authorization to board a plane; often required as proof of a flight taken when claiming missing credit.

BONUS: Miles accrued in excess of the actual mileage, which can include special promotions, class of service, and elite level allocations of extra miles.

BURN: Slang for redeeming your frequent flyer miles/points. Often teamed up with "Earn" as in Earn and Burn.

BUSINESS CLASS: Type of travel that denotes superior seating in a separate compartment on an aircraft between coach and first class. Opting for a seat in business class bestows passengers with extra baggage allowance and separate check-in. Most airline programs award bonus mileage for paid travel in business class.

CAPACITY CONTROLS: The process airlines, hotels and car rental agencies use to allocate awards depending on actual vs. anticipated demand. This term is often confused with "Blackout Dates."

CCL: Industry jargon for business class.

CERTIFICATE: An award voucher that a member must present at the redeeming company, such as a car rental company or hotel, or airline ticket counter.

CHECK-IN: To confirm intent to board a flight as booked by showing a ticket to an airline representative either at the ticket counter, curbside baggage check in or at the departure gate.

CLASS OF SERVICE: Refers generally to airline travel; indicates the level of travel, cabin position, size of seat and surrounding area, and amenities offered. Most common classifications are first class, business class and coach.

CO-BRANDED CARD: See "Affinity Card."

CODE SHARING: When one airline provides connecting service under another carrier's name. Both airlines' codes appear in reservation systems and on tickets. Code share flights occasionally accrue mileage.

COMBINING MILES: See "Pooling."

COMPANION TICKET: A free or discounted ticket for another person flying with a traveler who has purchased a ticket.

CONFIRMATION: An oral or written acknowledgment of a booking, subject to certain conditions.

CONFIRMED UPGRADE: Guarantees an upgrade to a higher class of service in advance of travel.

(IN) CONJUNCTION (WITH): The condition by which hotels and car rental agencies award bonus miles. For example, to accumulate America West mileage for a hotel stay at a Doubletree hotel, you must show your America West boarding pass as proof of flight in conjunction with the stay.

CONNECTION: Changing to a different airplane en route to a final destination. Connection bonuses and segment promotion credit are earned only if the connecting flight number is different from the origination flight number.

CONSOLIDATED MILEAGE MANAGERS: A service provided by a variety of travel- and financial-related Internet companies whereby miles and points accrued in several programs are listed in a single account statement.

COUPON BROKER: Travel agent who buys and sells frequent flyer award tickets—a practice prohibited by the airlines.

CURRENCY: Because frequent flyer miles/points number in the billions earned each year, it has often been observed that miles are like a "currency," second in value only to the U.S. dollar. It is true insofar as these miles/points have a major impact on the buying power of its members, whether for the more than 20 million free airline tickets awarded annually or toward the redemption of miles/points for a growing catalog of merchandise.

DIRECT FLIGHT: A flight with no change of plane; either a nonstop or a flight with one or more stops.

DISCOUNTED FARE: Usually refers to a "Restricted Fare." Be on the lookout for discounted coach fares that earn less than actual "flight miles" and that cannot be upgraded.

DOUBLE DIP: A hotel stay or airline flight that earns miles or points in two different loyalty programs simultaneously.

E-FARE: A specialty discount fare offered exclusively through the Internet; usually does not accrue miles.

EARN/BURN: Slang for mileage/points accrual and redemption.

ELECTRONIC UPGRADES (EGR): "Paperless" upgrades transacted solely through computers.

ELITE LEVEL: Additional services for members attaining certain levels of accrued miles or points. Elite level membership usually allows travelers to upgrade, accrue miles or points faster, and provides special check-in services, and grants special airline seating or hotel floors.

ELITE LEVEL BONUS: Miles or points earned in addition to actual mileage as a benefit of being an elite level member.

ELITE LEVEL UPGRADE: Upgrade to higher class of service available with membership in elite level programs.

ENHANCED: A term used in a derisory fashion by members of these programs for benefits removed by an airline, dressed up in a public relations spin as an "enhancement" to the program.

ENROLLMENT BONUS: A specific number of miles or points awarded upon first becoming a member of a program.

EQM: Elite Qualifying Miles. Many programs allow members to earn miles from a variety of activities, but generally, only miles earned through designated activities count toward the achievement of elite status. See also "Q Miles" and "Status Miles."

EUA: Continental and Northwest's Elite Upgrade Automation, which automatically upgrades elites to first class if seats are available.

EUG: Electronic upgrades.

EVIP: Refers to one-way, system-wide upgrades given to AA Executive Platinum elites. Such upgrades are "given" upon reaching Executive Platinum status.

EXP: Executive Platinum on American AAdvantage.

EXPEDITED AWARDS: Service offered by many programs for an additional cost, expedited awards allow members to speed up processing and delivery of award tickets or certificates. Often the requested award is delivered to members within 24 hours.

FAKE MILES: The currency—sometimes called miles, sometimes points—of credit cards with proprietary travel rewards programs. So called because there is no actual travel required (or measured) to earn rewards.

FAMILY ACCOUNT: See "Pooling."

FARE BASIS: Determines how miles or points are awarded based on the fare paid. For example, to accumulate mileage on some airlines, you must pay a published "Full Fare" rate. Some hotels require that you pay corporate rates or higher to accrue points. See "Qualifying Fares."

FCL: Industry jargon for first class.

FF: Frequent Flyer. Also VFF, a Very Frequent Flyer.

FFP: Frequent Flyer Program

FIRST CLASS: Separate compartment at the front of an aircraft with superior seating, service and amenities, free drinks and movies, separate check-in, and extra baggage allowance. Most airline programs award bonus mileage for travel in first class.

FLIGHT MILES: See "Actual Miles."

FOC: This dreaded disease is considered contagious by members of frequent flyer programs who choose to redeem their miles and benefits for upgrades rather than free awards. The disease is FOC—Fear of Coach. Also industry jargon for free, as in free of charge.

FREQUENT BUYERS: Frequent-traveler program members who earn most of their miles or points from credit card purchases or partner services rather than from frequent flying.

FULL FARE: A type of airline fare that is free of most restrictions (for example, advance purchase, Saturday night stay, non-refundable and non-endorsable). Full fares are more expensive and generally earn more elite qualifying miles. Contrast with "Restricted Fare."

FULL FOLIO: When a hotel program awards miles based on the amount spent for all hotel charges, including room service, gift shop purchases and like expenses.

GP: Gold Passport, the Hyatt Hotel Corporation's frequent stay program.

HK49s: United's confirmable North American upgrade certificates, good for travel within the 49 United States, the Caribbean, Canada or Mexico. This upgrade is not valid on flights to/from Hawaii, except when member is a resident of Hawaii. You may use Confirmed System Wide Upgrades anywhere United flies.

HoKeY: Widely used term by Continental flyers. These are the three types of coach fare codes that allow upgrades.

IN CONJUNCTION WITH: The restriction that hotels and car rental agencies apply when awarding miles. For example, to accumulate Mexicana Frecuenta mileage for a stay at a Camino Real hotel, you must show your Mexicana boarding pass as proof of a flight within a certain time period (usually 24 hours) of the stay.

INCENTIVE MILES: Miles purchased from an airline program by a company to be given to employees or customers as rewards.

LATINPASS: In 2000, this Latin American airline alliance gained notoriety when it sponsored one of the most lucrative promotions to date. The promotion gave members the opportunity to earn 1 million miles for a minimal amount of partner usage. LatinPass was overwhelmed by the number of participants. To this day, LatinPass is synonymous with irresistible, yet error-plagued promotions.

LINKED ACCOUNTS: When two members of a program either earn miles or points in the same account or when they can transfer miles between their two separate accounts; usually involves an affinity card.

MEMBERSHIP PRIVILEGES: Special privileges granted by airlines and hotels to members of frequent travel programs. For example, hotels may offer discounted rates or free nights to program members for a limited time.

MILEAGE CONVERSION: The exchange of miles or points from one program into another (think currency conversion). Conversion is possible through Points.com, Diners Club Rewards and Hilton HHonors.

MILEAGE JUNKIE: A frequent flyer who obsessively accumulates miles and points but often does not redeem many awards.

MILEAGE MANIAC: See "Mileage Junkie."

MILEAGE PURCHASE: The capability to purchase a certain percentage of miles needed to redeem a specific award.

MILEAGE RUN: A series of flights taken in a very short amount of time, solely for the purpose of accumulating frequent flyer miles, with a blatant disregard for the destinations.

MINIMUM MILEAGE: Minimum number of miles earned by program members regardless of the length of the flight.

MR: Membership Rewards, the program linked to American Express rewards cards.

NONSTOP: A flight that does not stop en route. A nonstop flight is always direct, but a direct flight is not always nonstop.

OFF-PEAK TRAVEL: Travel at a particular time of year when airlines predict a lower demand for seats. This usually excludes the time surrounding major holidays. Airlines designate specific peak and off-peak dates, and many do not allow award travel during peak times.

ONE CLASS: Usually associated with airline and car rental upgrades, allowing one level of service upgrade. For example, a one-class airline upgrade from coach to business class. Contrast this with a first-class upgrade jumping several classes of service from coach to first class.

ONLINE BONUSES: Miles/points earned through Internet transactions, whether by purchasing tickets or items or logging activity on a specific Web site.

OPAQUE FARES: Rates charged for airline tickets or hotel stays by deep discount "name your price" retailers such as Priceline and Hotwire. The fares are opaque in the sense that travelers commit to buying before they are told which airline or hotel is offering the deal they have chosen. Opaque fares do not earn frequent flyer miles or hotel points.

OPEN JAW: A roundtrip ticket with an open segment. For example, a routing from Chicago to New York, returning to Chicago from Boston. Open jaws are often allowed when flying on an award ticket and are often counted as a stopover.

PAPER UPGRADES: Certificates or vouchers that can physically be given to a check-in agent to claim an upgrade.

PARTNER: Two programs joining together to allow members to accrue miles or points in one or both programs. Also may allow members to use accumulated miles or points to redeem awards. Partners may be accrual partners only, award partners only or both.

PER NIGHT: When a hotel program awards miles/points for each night's accommodation.

PER STAY: When a hotel program awards miles/points once per visit, whether or not the visit comprises more than one night.

POINT CEILING: A limit on the amount of miles/points that can be earned through a specific method, such as an affinity card or a special bonus offer.

POOLING (MEMBERS): When two members combine miles or points from different accounts to redeem an award. Usually not allowed, but sometimes pooling is permissible for family members or spouses.

POOLING (PROGRAMS): When a member of two separate programs combines miles or points from both programs to claim an award with either program.

PRE-REGISTER: When a program requires a member to notify the program of the member's intent to earn a bonus prior to accrual. For example, if a bonus is offered for flying a specific route, the member must notify the program that the member is flying that itinerary to earn the bonus. If the program is not notified previous to the flight, it will not award the bonus. Often involves a promotion code.

PUDDING GUY: David Phillips, aka "The Pudding Guy," was made famous by FlyerTalk.com when he purchased over 12,000 packages of Healthy Choice pudding at 25 cents a pop to earn over a million frequent flyer miles.

PURCHASED UPGRADES: An upgrade to a higher class of service that can be obtained by currency.

Q MILES: Qualifying miles that count toward reaching Elite status with any airline, for example, not inclusive of any elite or class of service bonus, which often are not counted toward Elite level. See also "EQM" and "Status Miles."

QUALIFYING FARE or RATE: The airline fare or hotel or rental car rates that earn miles or points.

RECIPROCAL: When a partnership allows members from both programs to earn miles, redeem miles, or do both on the partner airline.

REDEEM/REDEMPTION: Cashing in miles or points for awards. See "Burn."

RESTRICTED FARE: Fares targeted at leisure travelers willing to accept heavy restrictions in return for discounted rates. They must be purchased at least seven days in advance, and more often 14 or 21 days. A Saturday night stay may be required (although this condition increasingly is being dropped). In the event of a flight disruption, the tickets cannot be used on another airline (they are non-endorsable).

RETROACTIVE CREDIT: Miles or points awarded to new members who may have flown or stayed previous to enrollment in a program. Requires proof of flight (boarding pass) or proof of stay (hotel receipt). Varies by program.

REWARD: See "Award."

RTW: Around-the-world, referring either to a fare or to the trip itself.

SEGMENT: One or more legs of continuous travel.

SERVICE CENTER: Place where members of frequent travel programs can call for award travel, redemption, accrual and current special promotion information.

SHARED ACCOUNT: When two separate members earn miles or points into a single account; usually involves an affinity card.

SPAV: Abbreviation for space available.

SPG: Starwood Preferred Guest.

STANDBY UPGRADE: Available at check-in if space is available in a higher class of service. Usually passengers check in no more than two hours in advance for standby upgrades.

STATUS: See "Elite Level."

STATUS MILES: Miles that count toward reaching elite status with any airline, for example, not inclusive of any elite or class of service bonus, which often are not counted toward elite level. See also "Q Miles" and "EQM."

STOPOVER: An intentional interruption of routing. Stopovers are sometimes allowed when flying on an award ticket. Length of stopover varies by airline.

SWU: Acronym for System Wide Upgrade. An upgrade award that can be used on any segment in an airline's route system. Many of the major airlines offer SWUs as a benefit to their elite level members.

THRESHOLD BONUS: A mileage/ points bonus incentive offered to members to fly or stay a predetermined number of miles or nights, and award bonus miles or points to members who reach threshold levels.

UNRESTRICTED FARE: See "Full Fare."

UPGRADE: Transferring to a better class of service or accommodations, such as from coach to first class. Upgrades may be one class upgrades (see "One Class") or jump several classes of service.

VIPOW: One-way complimentary system wide upgrade certificate on American Airlines. Executive Platinum members receive such certificates each year that they attain/retain this highest level of elite status with American.

WALK-UP FARE: See "Full Fare."

YCL: Industry jargon for coach/ economy class.

YMMV: Your Mileage May Vary.

 Randy Petersen

This Monday through Friday, Randy Petersen will receive 4,000 e-mails (that is 800 each day!); do 12 newspaper, TV, magazine or radio interviews; peruse 27 magazines; talk to the managers of 15 different frequent flyer programs; and review the bonus offerings of more than 130 of these programs. This will be a slow week.

As a former marketing and merchandise presentation manager for a large menswear retailer, Randy spent much of his time flying and keeping accurate records of his mileage awards. Nearly everyone he knew would go to him for frequent flyer advice. When it got to the point of constantly advising people, Randy started his own frequent flyer information business, which now includes *InsideFlyer* magazine (the leading publication in the world about frequent traveler programs) and FlyerTalk.com. Randy's favorite effort has been the launch of the Mileage Donation Center (www.miledonor.com), which helps people donate unused miles to charitable groups.

The Wall Street Journal refers to Randy as "... the most influential frequent flyer in America" and *The New York Times* tagged him as "the world's leading expert on airline frequent flyer programs." Randy has been named to the "Frequent Traveler Hall of Fame" sponsored by the Hilton Hotel Corporation and has been named "One of the 25 Most Influential Executives in the Business Travel Industry" by *Business Travel News*. Randy has appeared on CBS, NBC, ABC News Radio, Good Morning America and European Business News. He is frequently quoted in *The Wall Street Journal, USA Today, The New York Times* and more than 100 other newspapers and magazines.

Randy currently resides on a ranch outside of Colorado Springs, Colorado, but maintains a very active schedule of worldwide business travels. His outside activities include snow skiing, water sports, reading, renovating houses and playing basketball.

Tim Winship

Tim Winship is a nationally known authority on the travel industry and frequent flyer programs. His 20-year travel industry career includes loyalty-marketing management assignments with Singapore Airlines, All Nippon Airways and The Hilton Hotel Corporation. During his tenure, he developed new frequent flyer programs (Goldpass and ANA Mileage Club), managed existing programs, and designed and implemented reward promotions.

In 1997, Tim launched FrequentFlier.com, a Web site devoted to helping travelers choose, use and understand frequent flyer programs. And in 1998, he began publishing a weekly e-newsletter, The FrequentFlier Crier. The Web site and e-newsletter have won many awards including the BOOT (Best of Online Travel) award that reflects the opinions of more than one million online voters, as well as being featured in the current edition of McGraw-Hill's *Guide to 500 Best Aviation Web Sites* and *net.people* published by CyberAge Books. In addition to his own publications, Tim is a contributing editor for *Frequent Flyer* magazine and SmarterTravel.com. He also writes the syndicated monthly newspaper column, "The Extra Mile."

His advice and analysis is regularly sought and cited by *The New York Times, USA Today, The Wall Street Journal* and CNN. Tim is a member of the Society of American Travel Writers and a longtime supporter of the Frequent Travel Marketing Association. He earned an M.B.A. in marketing from the University of Southern California. Tim also holds a B.F.A. in design from California Institute of the Arts, and has completed several years of graduate work in philosophy and symbolic logic at California State University, Los Angeles.

Tim lives in Los Angeles where he has a choice of three airports: Los Angeles International, Burbank and Long Beach.